W9-CNL-179

THE LITERACY PRINCIPAL

Leading, supporting, and assessing reading and writing initiatives

2nd Edition

David Booth
Jennifer Rowsell

FOREWORD BY
Michael Fullan

Stenhouse Publishers
Portland, Maine
www.stenhouse.com

Pembroke Publishers Limited
Markham, Ontario
www.pembrokepublishers.com

To
Jay and Katie
Madeleine and Fred

Pembroke Publishers
538 Hood Road
Markham, Ontario, Canada L3R 3K9
www.pembrokepublishers.com

Published in the U.S. by Stenhouse Publishers
480 Congress Street
Portland, ME 04101
www.stenhouse.com

We acknowledge the financial support of the Government of Canada through the Book Publishing Industry Development Program (BPIDP) for our publishing activities.

We acknowledge the Government of Ontario through the Ontario Media Development Corporation's Ontario Book Initiative.

Author Acknowledgments and Credits

We would like to express our deep gratitude to all of the contributors to our book, from both Canada and the United States, for their wise insights and comprehensive knowledge about literacy leadership in our schools. We have included the excellent books and articles they have written in Resources page 150 as recommended reading.

As well, we are grateful to the Ontario Ministry of Education and to the Literacy and Numeracy Secretariat under the leadership of Avis Glaze, Chief Achievement Officer, for the educational reports and publications referenced in this book.

Article pages 30–32, "Nine Areas of Content Knowledge" from *For Principals: A Blueprint for Literacy Leadership* at http://www.cliontheweb.org/principals_blueprint.html. Reprinted by permission of the Children's Literacy Initiative.

Article on page 119 "Testing the Unseen Curriculum" by Catherine Mulroney in the *Toronto Star*, May 13, 2002. Reprinted by permission of Catherine Mulroney.

Excerpt on page 130 from *Conversations: Strategies for Teaching, Learning and Evaluation* by Regie Routman. Copyright 2000. Reprinted by permission of Heinemann.

Library and Archives Canada Cataloguing in Publication

Booth, David W. (David Wallace)
    The literacy principal : leading, supporting and assessing reading and writing initiatives / David Booth and Jennifer Rowsell. — 2nd ed.

Includes bibliographical references and index.
ISBN 978-1-55138-216-6

  1. Reading. 2. English language—Rhetoric—Study and teaching.
I. Rowsell, Jennifer. II. Title.

LB1576.B68 2007   428.4071   C2007-904163-9

Editor: Kat Mototsune
Cover Design: John Zehethofer
Typesetting: Jay Tee Graphics Ltd.

Printed and bound in Canada
9 8 7 6 5 4 3 2

Contents

12 Steps toward Literacy Success…

1. Understand the theory and research on how literacy develops in young people.

2. Ensure that students read for meaning and find significance in their reading in every curriculum area.

3. Model and demonstrate literacy strategies to support and encourage developing readers.

4. Include a wide variety of reading resources — different styles, genres, and formats, including new technology, in all curriculum areas.

5. Encourage students to talk with others about what they are reading in order to build background and expand comprehension.

6. Guide students to reread and to respond in ways that are meaningful to them.

7. Connect writing and reading, so that students learn to "read as writers," and to "write as readers."

8. Incorporate graphic organizers to help students to interact with their reading, and record and organize their thinking about texts.

9. Help students to see themselves as successful readers, growing in confidence and competence, and setting goals to increase literacy achievement.

10. Lead students to a better understanding of how different text forms work, the characteristics, qualities, and vocabulary that are specific to each type of text they will meet.

11. Develop a literacy mandate for the entire school, with teams of teachers engaged in building competent readers and writers.

12. Celebrate literacy every day in every curriculum area by increasing and expanding school resources — books, magazines, technology, and the library.

Foreword

If you had to name one thing that every school should do well, you would have to consider teaching deep literacy as standing head and shoulders over all other priorities. It is the key to every student's future. Therefore, the main role of the principal is to mobilize everyone — teachers, parents, students — to make literacy happen. In this new edition of *The Literacy Principal*, David Booth and Jennifer Rowsell tell us in vivid detail how we should go about this joyful task.

It is all here: creating a culture of literacy, which means creating a learning community specializing in literacy; understanding literacy principles and practices, which means that students and teachers grasp and truly understand the bases of literacy; creating literacy success, which includes the myriad strategies for making literacy permeate daily practice; assessing from the inside out, which reminds us that good evaluation *is* learning and is tantamount to being accountable to ourselves and the public.

The book is full of vignettes from teachers, principals, and other leaders. Booth and Rowsell make it clear that the literacy principal mandates helping others find literacy wherever it is. And the authors find it everywhere. They cover meaning, spelling, play, novels, technology, writing, all types of text, skills, and more. Most of all, they show us how to infuse the entire formal and informal school culture with rich literacy experiences that link to the daily lives of all. They make literacy meaningful and central to our lives, now and in the future. *The Literacy Principal* once again models ways for us to pursue literacy naturally but deliberately. This is not curriculum implementation and testing as dry, rational work. It is the joy of learning.

In revising *The Literacy Principal*, David Booth and Jennifer Rowsell bring to life in one place what many of us have been doing for the past five years in large systems: namely, accomplishing widespread improvement in literacy learning by raising the bar and closing the gap for all students. In our recent book, *Breakthrough*,* Peter Hill, Carmel Crevola, and I make the case for focusing on the "precision, personalization and professional learning of teachers" — individual attention to the learning needs of each child, precise instructional response that meets that need, and teachers learning every day how to do this with the help of educational and administrative leaders. Carol Rolheiser, Bill Hogarth, Lyn Sharratt, and I have been working in partnership with leaders and teachers in the 175 schools (including the 32 high schools) of the York Region District School Board. We have made big steps forward in Ontario by focusing explicitly on literacy in all 72 districts and all 4000 elementary schools in a Literacy/Numeracy Strategy that has positively affected thousands of students and teachers.

---

* Fullan, M.; Hill, P. and Crevola, C. (2006) *Breakthrough* Thousand Oaks, CA: Corwin Press; and Toronto, ON: Ontario Principals Council.

In short, literacy has momentum, but much more remains to be done. *The Literacy Principal* inspires us to get on with it, as it helps show what this journey looks like in practice and how to get more of it.

Michael Fullan, Professor Emeritus
Ontario Institute for Studies in Education
University of Toronto

Introduction:
Leading from Within and Without

Principal Principal stormed into our art room yesterday, smelling pleasure. His mustache moved up and down, a radar sweep for all things unruly. An unseen hand turned off the radio as he crossed the threshold, and bags of potato chips vanished, leaving the faint scent of salt to mix with vermillion oil paint and wet clay.

He scanned the room for merriment. Found only bowed heads, graceful pencils, dipping brushes. Principal Principal stalked out of the room.

Maybe I'll be an artist if I grow up.

Laurie Halse Anderson, *Speak*, Farrar, Straus and Giroux, 1999.

Welcome to the new version of *The Literacy Principal.* The first change you might notice is the cover; like the rest of the revision, it represents the new developments in school leadership, especially in literacy. Instead of a solitary principal loaded with books, the cover shows the whole school represented as the agent of literacy change, situated in an imagined space at the centre of the community. The book connects to everything in our children's lives that affects their literacy growth: within school, and outside of school in the home and the community. Today, the principal's role is much more that of a mediator and animator, helping establish conditions that can move toward supporting all children's expectations and possibilities as literate humans.

In the past six years, much has happened in school leadership locally and globally. The New Literacies movement has emerged as a way of recognizing the outside-to-inside impact of education, both formal and informal, on a child's life. Coaching and mentoring are front and centre in helping teachers change and adapt to the new information and technology that are available in literacy education. Professional development has become continuous, rather than a series of one-time experiences, in both schools and districts, and in provinces and states. New initiatives have been developed to help educators create a literate and responsible citizenry. Most of all, principals are ever more integral to the success of school literacy teams.

We recognize the changes that the last few years have brought about, in that school administrators have developed their own professional standards and applied them to a wider frame of reference for their schools' literacy success. In writing this book, we have included the views of many well-respected educators about what makes an effective school leadership team.

We know that an effective principal understands the particular community that situates his or her school. We know the role of technology has changed the face of literacy forever, and that technology has increased the range of possibilities. As educators, we are working toward understanding the nuances of gender issues in both the resources we choose and the types of activities we create. We know and appreciate new textual forms, their origins, and their functions. We have widened our lens to include all subjects and their literacy constructs because form and function have always mattered. We know that assessment is connected to the whole program that a school develops, not just to the results of one set of tests; however, we recognize that the information gleaned from tests can help us fill out the picture of each child's progress.

These shifts in the leadership and literacy landscape have been supported by informed international research projects that have strengthened our understanding about literacy and our knowledge about students learn as readers and writers.

As we noted in the original *Literacy Principal*, educators face several challenges in promoting a strong literacy program in their schools: test scores; the public sharing of test results; literacy difficulties with students; class sizes; the increasing role of technology; resources for students with diverse needs; and parents' demands and expectations for their children. We hope that this revised edition supports some of these developments. A constant is that literacy is at the heart of the learning process. There is no quick fix to a literacy concern — literacy is as individual as each student, and no one test or published program is the answer. Nonetheless, there are ways to contemporize leadership and build capacity in our schools based on what we know and what research has to offer.

As with the first edition, there are some guiding principles for school leaders that can form a framework for literacy-based school change:

- Create a shared literacy vision in your school that it is clear and shaped by the particularities of your school community.
- Understand the textual worlds of your students and the practices that accompany these texts; this entails showing your students that you understand and appreciate their communities.
- Work as a school literacy team, with everyone having a role in determining the vision and the implementation plan, each member bringing specific expertise to building the culture of literacy in the school.
- Build in time and opportunities for professional development for the stakeholders who are developing the program.
- Mediate the world outside of your school within your school; be aware of literacy in the community, global literacy initiatives, New Literacies, and the place of district implementation plans.

Principals make change happen when they open up their schools to change and foster a culture that mediates the children's lives in the community with classroom contexts. In seeking to create a literacy culture in a school, all members of a school's literacy team need to become researchers, making use of their own experiences as well as information in reports, professional articles, Internet sites, and books to gather data that can be analyzed. Making decisions about literacy initiatives then rests on interpreting the data in the context of a particular situation — the quicker everyone is in participating in this research process, the sooner the school can move into an action plan.

Challenging our personal assumptions is more important than ever in implementing change for success, and has become a strong theme in this book. For example, resistance to technology, given that many of us feel like "digital immigrants," may keep us from seeing that how we make meaning from specific genres of texts is quite different in some ways but remarkably similar in other ways. Exploring new forms and functions of the texts in our lives and in the future can change the way we lead and teach and understand.

As we have said, we need to ensure that every child in a school is developing as a literate person. On this journey, they need to see their classmates, their teachers, and their administrators as members of a literate community, open to incorporating the kinds of texts and responses necessary for literacy competence. All students need to feel what it is like to succeed in literacy.

We see this book as a series of conversations: between teachers and principals; between the two of us as authors committed to literacy education and to building capacity for fostering literate lives in school; between the authors and you, the reader. At the end of each chapter, in boxes within the text, and in the margins and open spaces in the book, we provide voices of researchers and scholars who work in literacy education and who have contributed important perspectives on improving literacy for all.

The Literacy Principal is the focus of our studies, but the school literacy team is the heart of the reading/writing culture in a school. How the principal leads the development of the school-wide literacy initiative will determine the effect of the process. We value the important roles of the school administrators, and we recognize the support required to ensure that the literacy mandate for their schools be fulfilled. We thank Michael Fullan for his insightful work in promoting the theory and practice of school change, and we are grateful to the principals and vice principals for their continuing growth as literacy leaders.

CHAPTER 1

Creating a Culture of Literacy in Your School

> Effective literacy teachers operate from a needs basis, yet they also must have a strong sense of what other supports would help them, so that they can draw on them and feed them into their practice. They can then use their professional knowledge and practice base to help guide their literacy teaching at any point in the day.
>
> Carol Rolheiser

There are mounting pressures and expectations for schools to ensure that *all* students are acquiring the literacy skills they need to succeed in the future. As urban centres expand and immigration increases, there are growing numbers of students who are new to the country and who speak English as a second language. As a result, teachers are more beholden than ever before to provide literacy instruction that sets the groundwork for successful futures for our children. Support networks required to develop students' skills need to always be in place.

With the vast amount of theory and research available in the area of literacy and language development, there is certainly no lack of information, resources, and materials in place to ensure success for all. Yet, sometimes schools still fall short of set standards and often fail to meet struggling students' needs for intensive literacy teaching. At the same time, school districts grapple with how to channel their mandate to improve students' literacy rates into a solid, unified, and thorough vision with practical classroom strategies to implement such a vision. Ultimately, districts are limited by the amount of time, staff, and resources they have at their disposal.

It is precisely for these reasons that districts and governments have committed to "literacy for all" as a key goal for their schools. With "literacy for all" as a district-wide mandate, it is necessary for teachers, school leaders, and district and government officials to allot more time in the curriculum for literacy development *and* to have more access to best-practice examples of excellence in literacy teaching. What this entails is a greater understanding of what creates literacy-based school change, or more specifically, what creates changes in literacy standards and practices on the part of educational stakeholders. To achieve this, it is imperative that districts have access to research and information about the experience of other schools and other districts undertaking to improve their teaching of literacy.

As it stands, there is little research exploring the context of literacy-based school change. According to three field-based research reports, with Carol Rolheiser, the associate dean of OISE/UT, as the lead writer of the research teams:

There has been little exploration of the challenges and accelerators facing schools and districts as they attempt to improve their teaching of literacy. At the moment, there is a void in the literature vis-à-vis how schools are working toward creating improvements in literacy teaching and learning.

See Literacy-Based Change in Schools by Carol Rolheiser and Karen Edge on page 28.

Rolheiser and her teams identified five categories of change factors as fundamental and foundational to literacy-based school change:

- Principal leadership
- Teachers' knowledge, skills, and dispositions
- Professional community
- Program coherence
- Technical resources

Some of the issues at the heart of literacy-driven school change appear to be the following: How can schools change their infrastructure and classroom programs to improve student literacy achievement? With a strong literacy initiative in place, how can schools move forward? What can school leaders and their literacy teams do to bring about such changes?

Researchers and scholars clearly identify the important role of early literacy in the lives of children. Of all subject areas, literacy stands as one of the most effective vehicles for school change, in that success in literacy ensures success in other curriculum areas. That is, if students can read, write, and talk effectively, they can participate more fully in other areas of learning.

Research shows that intensive early literacy initiatives in schools and districts result in higher levels of achievement in all areas of the curriculum. Alongside higher achievement levels in other subject areas, literacy initiatives create a greater nexus between home and school. Part and parcel of early literacy programs and initiatives is involving parents in their children's literacy development by having them read to their children at home and build environments conducive to literacy success.

Studies on school change demonstrate that, although system-wide changes in policy and programs are important for large-scale change to occur, building the capacity for change in individual schools is essential to effective school reform. Rolheiser explains:

Where schools have built teachers' knowledge, skills and dispositions, where they have created a professional community, where the programs have coherence and focus, where teachers' work is supported by appropriate resources, and where the leadership exists to both lead and support the work of the school, there we find improvements in school achievement.

This is quite a list of demands, but when we create a school culture that believes in a professional community, that has a strong, coherent vision, that spends money on useful resources, and, above all else, that constructs a leadership team standing behind a literacy-based school, we build the groundwork for effective literacy initiatives.

The Leadership Role

Michael Fullan refers to leadership as the driving force behind change taking place in schools, and our discussion of literacy-based school change pivots on leadership. If there is one message we wish to send out it is that shifts in literacy teaching and learning have less to do with new information about literacy and much more to do with changes in the infrastructure of schools.

We have already touched on the central role of the principal as a lead voice in literacy initiatives. Schools that have successful literacy programs show evidence of strong principal leadership, with focused attention on setting a literacy agenda, supporting teachers, accessing resources, and building a capacity for further growth.

Principals often plan, launch, and monitor the creation of a school vision and explicitly or implicitly establish a school culture by encouraging collaborative efforts among colleagues, facilitating professional development, and focusing on school strategies to improve standards. As will be discussed in more detail shortly, leadership tends to flourish when it is shared. While the principal choreographs shared leadership, it is important to acknowledge and encourage individuals in leadership positions within the school.

Principals as Instructional Leaders

To effectively plan, launch, and monitor a literacy initiative or support others in this endeavor, principals need an interest in and even a passion for literacy, alongside a knowledge base about literacy and language development. Like teachers, principals increasingly wear a number of hats. There is no doubt that this multitude of roles can pull a school leader away from an instructional framework and more into administrative duties and management tasks.

However, programs and initiatives that assist principals in generating and maintaining teacher enthusiasm for improving literacy instruction are essential elements of school literacy improvement. Therefore, principals need to enrich their own understanding of exemplary teaching strategies, materials, and assessment and evaluation techniques.

Principals as Facilitators of Professional Development

Principals who believe in and even feel passionately about a project initiative infuse momentum and purpose into its goals. Clear communication about project goals, literacy plans and policies, and professional development events helps keep everyone on track. Communicating goals to the group compels individual teachers and teaching teams to maintain a commitment to literacy initiatives and to improve literacy standards in a school.

The act of negotiating district-wide demands with teacher needs in professional development is a skill principals need to hone in order to effectively lead a literacy initiative.

Sharing the Leadership Roles

Principals who share the responsibility of leadership are much more successful at creating positive change for teachers and students. The more evidence there is of teamwork in a school, the more significant the change in literacy standards.

See Nine Areas of Content Knowledge from the Children's Literacy Initiative on page 30.

Shelley Harwayne enjoyed acting as a substitute teacher in her school, when, for example, a teacher wanted to attend a professional development session. She was always prepared with a read-aloud selection from her own collection. She believes that principals are teachers and that literacy is a significant part of that role.

"We talked to teachers and grade team teachers, inviting them in one by one, to discover their strengths, what was needed as professional development, and where they saw themselves in the school in the future. We also revisited school plans so that we would be able to identify where our needs were and where we could set appropriate goals and targets. The board has targets that offer models: we considered our population of students and then set goals to meet those board-wide targets over time."
— Steven Reid

As Carol Rolheiser notes about teacher commitment to a literacy initiative, "This is of great value in times of leadership shortages as it serves to create a great cadre of teachers with leadership experiences within schools."

Shared leadership builds an environment that supports planning time and collaboration, that contributes to evenly parceling out leadership positions. The more leadership you give to teachers, the greater will be the teacher "buy-in" and commitment to a literacy project or initiative.

A few models of shared leadership that have proven effective in supporting literacy-based school change are described below.

SCHOOL-BASED LEADERSHIP TEAMS

Some districts have developed a literacy support structure by creating leadership teams to build capacity at the school level. The effect of this model is greatly determined by the training team members receive in building a collaborative work culture dependent upon each school's context, so that they can sustain innovation and promote continuous improvement. Since the teams are largely composed of teachers, along with an administrator, the members need time to plan together to determine their course of action and to target specific improvements for their school. As well, these teams are strengthened by district support such as professional development sessions and summer institutes, where they can be part of a network of educators, sharing information and strategies from the different schools involved in a literacy project.

TEACHER LEADERS

Some schools rely on teacher leaders in order to support literacy change. This model works in a school culture that is collegial and professional, and where teachers take responsibility for their own growth as educators and for changing the learning conditions in their school. It is necessary for those involved to be able to learn from other colleagues with similar status, in order to develop their expertise as a cohesive school community. Teacher leaders need to be able to understand the needs of and the varied competencies that different staff members bring to each of their classrooms, and to foster literacy change according to individual professional needs. Most important, teacher leaders need the support of their administration in working toward collaborative inquiry and professional growth.

LITERACY COACH/COORDINATOR

See The Literacy Coach by Enrique A. Puig and Kathy S. Froelich on page 32; Being a Literacy Coach by Lea Pelletier on page 35; and From Student Response to Effective Literacy Teaching by Jeannie Wilson on page 38.

With some literacy initiatives, the administrative team comprises the principal as provider of support and mentorship and a literacy coordinator as a liaison with teaching staff and as a resident expert on literacy teaching and learning. The literacy coordinator role is central to the planning, monitoring, and implementing of literacy-based school change. The literacy coordinator not only organizes professional development sessions for staff, but also sets up and maintains a literacy resource room for teachers to visit when they need support in their literacy teaching. Literacy coordinators plan cooperatively with teachers and promote team work in meeting the targets of their school. In addition, literacy coordinators take on the following responsibilities:

- Assist teachers in developing and maintaining classroom materials
- Work closely with intervention support, such as the Reading Recovery™ teacher
- Connect theory and classroom practice
- Coordinate data collection

- Mentor teachers by providing support, direction, and assistance to meet individual needs
- Engage, influence, and motivate staff to explore all areas of literacy
- Coordinate regular meetings to discuss progress on initiatives

Like teacher leaders, literacy coordinators drive change in schools by disseminating literacy information and inciting enthusiasm about improving students' reading and writing.

Keeping Teachers Up-to-Date

In order to create literate schools, principals and leadership teams must ensure that teachers have the knowledge, skills, and dispositions to not only choose effective teaching strategies or assessment strands but, more importantly, to have the wherewithal to do so. That teachers strongly benefit from such professional development, and that this has an impact on student achievement, has been proven time and time again. A teacher's professional knowledge is a key ingredient in a teacher's success with students.

What tends to be undermined in the triad of knowledge, skills, and dispositions are the skills and dispositions required to effectively teach a core process like literacy. Building skills in lesson planning, in pedagogy, and in assessment and evaluation are as important as building dispositions to create change and higher expectations in students.

One of the more contentious areas in the field of literacy teaching is assessment and evaluation. Many of the schools implementing literacy initiatives differ in their approach to assessing reading and writing development. In Chapter 4 we offer a compendium of assessment approaches, but in terms of creating a literacy-based environment, we want to highlight the kaleidoscope of possible perspectives one can take on instituting effective assessment and evaluation.

Creating a Professional Community

Based on research and practice, successful schools have collaborative cultures in which administrators and teachers work as a team with a common commitment to literacy initiatives that ensure success for all. By creating a collaborative culture among educators on a literacy team, it is possible to incite interest in theory and new methodologies and practices in the area of literacy and language development. A collaborative culture naturally establishes partnerships with other possible team members, such as parents, in a common pursuit to improve literacy skills for all students.

See Lyn Sharratt's Lessons in Leading for Literacy on page 97.

It has been shown that if schools work as teams, there is much sharing of expertise so that all students benefit from the most effective literacy instruction available. To create a unified team committed to literacy-based school change, a school needs a specific, detailed, and rigorous literacy plan that has a shared vision of how it will get from here to there. Literacy-driven schooling unites staff, parents, and children by creating a culture of self-directed learning.

A collaborative culture provides a combination of pressure and support to help teachers deal with change and improve student learning. In *The New Meaning of Educational Change*, Michael Fullan describes this process as "the overlapping of strong pedagogical practice" married to the existence and implementation of assessment literacy. What is implicit in such a belief is that teachers need to work together with clear goals and, at the same time, with clear accountability. To move from a collaborative community to a professional community where teachers overlap strong pedagogy with assessment, teachers need the ability and desire to assess their students and to respond to the results of that assessment to inform their practice.

The students too need to be brought on board in creating successful literacy experiences. Paul Shaw envisions a school that believes in ranges and opportunities for choice across age groups. He points out that as children get older, their opportunities to choose diminish (i.e., the children who have the most choice are in Kindergarten). With such a revelation in mind, educators need to reevaluate their images of the learner. Principals not only need to create collaborative school environments that promote professional development so that teachers can hone their practice, but also facilitate self-directed learning so that students at all grade levels have more choice in their learning. By taking control of their own learning, students become more independent, are more in control, and ultimately make better choices in their learning.

What also lies at the heart of creating schools as professional communities is developing effective partnerships with parents. In Carol Rolheiser's studies, all the schools involved in her teams' research spoke of the difficulties in engaging their communities. Admittedly, each school saw community involvement as vital to the success of literacy initiatives, but most encountered obstacles in consolidating an equal commitment from the community. Those schools that managed to overcome this resistance and actively engage parents in literacy initiatives gained immeasurably.

There are several factors that have proven instrumental in rejuvenating support for literacy initiatives and creating a strong professional community, including

- space and time for change
- in-school professional development
- district professional development
- teacher motivation
- support systems for teachers
- the support of parents

Providing Space and Time for Learning

To create a culture of self-directed learning for both teachers and students, principals need to provide proper time and precious resources to allow all parties to thoroughly explore their needs and their interests in relation to literacy-based change. For teachers, time is a commodity. The reality in today's schools is that teachers often face 25 to 35 students during the day, and then spend time at the end of the day going over what happened in class and reflecting on student needs. There is rarely time in all of this to take part in formal professional development or to work alone or collaboratively on increasing knowledge and skills.

Teachers need both in-school and out-of-school time to work alone or collaboratively on fields of interest, to discuss and share ideas with others, as well as to advance their knowledge and skills. Appreciating the background and experience that teachers bring to the classroom is part of the process of creating

In Nova Scotia, as the literacy initiative moved up one grade at a time, the Department of Education sent to every teacher in that grade a large selection of books (mostly single copies, and some batches of five or six copies for small groups) appropriate to the interests and range of reading abilities of students in that grade. The books had been juried by both teachers and students before approval, and the response from classroom teachers was unalloyed delight.

Paul Shaw suggests that schools place professional development in the schedule and plan for a certain number of hours each year. He explains that providing time and space for professional development naturally creates a culture of change that is receptive to more inquiry and reflection.

literacy-based change. Where principals have made time for change, the result is often a more dedicated staff — the key to the success of any initiative.

Learning At and Around Your School

See Building Effective Mentoring Relationships by Jim Strachan on page 41.

Collaborative teaching and learning environments naturally infuse collegiality and cooperation with a desire for in-school professional development. Encouraging colleagues to pursue interests individually and to forge groups is part of a principal's job as the lead voice in literacy initiatives.

What distinguishes successful initiatives from others is the value they have placed on bringing teams of teachers together to create effective literacy-based school change. By working together to resolve challenges and issues around literacy teaching, teachers believe they can create partnerships and share practices. Welcoming, valuing, and respecting the expertise and views of other educators — whether they are fellow teachers or administrators — maximizes the use of in-school knowledge and capacity. Likewise, creating an instructional focus within schools fosters an overall commitment to literacy projects.

A clear focus on in-school professional development in the field of literacy and language education is a must if literacy success for all is going to be addressed — not just for teachers, but for the administrator too. Steven Reid explains why it is essential for school principals to be learners themselves and to model the importance of professional development:

> People will often notice when the principal spends time with literacy initiatives. Teachers, then, on the whole have a clearer understanding that school leaders are willing to work with them in any way that they can.

Learning Outside Your School

Marcelle Mayer wrote a weekly memo to all staff that began with an insightful quote of the week, and then went on to outline the upcoming week's events and to highlight thank-yous or celebrations of an individual teacher's work. As well, she always had a supply of beautiful stationery in her desk drawer and wrote personal notes to individual teachers, thanking them for their wonderful work in the classroom or in the larger school community.

In examining schools involved in major literacy initiatives, it is important to note that part of their success lies in the principals' support for off-site teacher professional development. Collaborative teams may be culled from across a district, or entire schools may attend district-wide training sessions where grade teams have opportunities to voice specific issues, concerns, reflections, and questions.

Exposure to such training creates a common language and a forum where staff members and other participants can voice their questions and concerns. In this way, district professional development facilitates built-in support from the district itself, as well as from teachers at other schools.

Principals and other literacy leaders, such as literacy coordinators/coaches, can also benefit greatly from bringing their strengths to the table at district-wide sessions, and then using or sharing the knowledge and skills gained back at their schools. As Carol Rolheiser observes:

> The project moved them outside their own schools, to understand how others were seeing some of the problems, and to learn the strategies that others were using. For example, the principals delved into issues that they might worry about as administrators in their schools — things that may be more difficult to delegate. The literacy coordinators focused much more specifically on the content of literacy.

Motivating Teachers

Teachers have an immense amount of work and, generally speaking, at times feel undervalued and underappreciated. The problem of teacher motivation grows along with the students: for high-school teachers, the number of students they teach per day can range from 100 (small school with four classes/day) to 180 or more (larger school with five classes/day). Add to this the fact that at semestered high schools, many teachers have no preparation periods at all for a full semester (half the school year) at a time. Principals have to be aware of waning enthusiasm and, indeed, be mindful of not only building future success for their students, but also for their staff.

Part of building a successful future for teachers involves creating an incentive for them to build on their own teaching practice, thereby fostering improvement in student achievement. Time and professional development are two key pieces in the puzzle to increasing teachers' job professionalism and satisfaction. Lea Pelletier writes,

> Time and professional development are often the first things to go in a pinch. Our rural schools face the problem of finding substitute teachers: subs tend to move to cities where there are many schools so they don't have to travel an hour or more to get to the job. When there are not enough substitutes to cover teachers away due to illness, other teachers take the sick teachers' classes on their preparation periods. Often, this means teachers who have been booked to attend regional professional development simply cannot go.

But a principal's commitment to teacher professional development reaps its rewards in teacher motivation. Imbuing enthusiasm for teaching and building in time to reflect on their own successes gives teachers more perspective on their own growth. After some professional development and collaboration with colleagues, teachers usually begin to witness changes in their teaching practice and in their students' reading and writing achievement. These are landmark events, as they make much of the process seem tangible and thereby worthwhile.

Although literacy initiatives can add to teacher workload, they often demonstrate that time invested in development and growth in practice leads to more fulfillment and, to some extent, enjoyment in teaching because there are demonstrated results. The positive feedback and results derived from their new sets of skills have proven to motivate teachers.

Supporting Teachers

There are a variety of ways that a principal can set up strong literacy-based support systems for teachers in a school. One way, as described earlier, is to appoint a literacy coordinator whose job it is to support teachers in implementing exemplary literacy programs.

A key ingredient in the success of major initiatives has been the role of a literacy coordinator as a resident authority and overall support to staff. With a literacy coordinator in place, teachers can benefit from a library of resources, supplemental readings to clarify or add to a teacher's knowledge of key components of literacy teaching, useful teaching demonstrations, and, on the whole, a clearer instructional program.

In studies on literacy-based school change, teachers mention that they are better teachers of literacy and that they are more aware of effective literacy-specific teaching strategies once they have witnessed successes in their classrooms.

"Do you know, in your school, who the struggling readers are? Do you know who the successful readers and writers are? Do you know why? Do you know who the teachers are on your staff who are really successful teachers in literacy? Do you know how to forge networks that let that expertise be shared? Asking and reflecting upon these types of questions leads the way to a school culture with literacy front and centre." — Kathryn Broad

In many cases, although teachers have the knowledge base and even access to resources for effective literacy programs, they do not always have the time to keep abreast of new trends or to update their libraries. With a literacy coordinator at hand, teachers have daily access to resources, are assisted in their classroom when the need arises, and have a resource person in place to enable them to work quickly on areas of their teaching that may need improvement.

Supporting Parents

For literacy teaching to be effective, there has to be both centripetal and centrifugal forces in which students' home literacy experiences are brought into the classroom and in-school literacy events and practices are taken back home. In short, the home–school nexus is vital to a successful project or initiative.

Involvement may take the form of parental participation in classroom or school events, such as author days or literacy nights, as well as parental input at home by following up on reading and writing activities, and, of course, reading to children every day. Many teachers have commented on the fact that strategies for reading are easily shared with parents and that this enables them to give parents clear and simple techniques to use when reading with their children.

In Steven Reid's school, the literacy team designed a program for at-risk readers in Grades 1, 2, and 3. In this program, throughout the year, the staff phoned parents, advising them of ideas for supporting literacy with their children and helping them locate inexpensive reading materials to bring into their homes to support literacy with their children every day.

Several of the schools in one successful district-wide literacy project had literacy nights where parents become more informed about the goals of the project and listened to success stories. Literacy initiatives have also served as a bridge in communities in which many of the students' parents were learning English themselves and could benefit from programs in place at schools. Another way to contact parents about literacy is the school newsletter.

Developing an Effective Literacy Program

Program coherence or consistency is key to effectively implementing a literacy initiative. Having said that, creating coherence in a large and diverse district is no easy task. Principals are given the unwieldy task of conciliating the multitudinous needs of teachers and students with policies mandated from the district or state/province. One of the ways to make the task manageable is to create coherence through a specific and detailed literacy plan. In addition, professional development, the cornerstone of any initiative, can be orchestrated by a literacy coordinator or members of a teaching staff.

With the increasing workload of teachers and the constant threat of policy fragmentation, principals and their staffs need to have a clear sense of how their own programs relate to the whole (i.e., how their school literacy policy matches policy mandates). However, this cannot be at the expense of meeting the needs of each micro-community — a literacy framework must have the latitude to accommodate the specific needs of individual staffs and students. Schools that have created goals based on the needs of their own school, as well as district and state/provincial mandates, have experienced a much smoother implementation curve. By creating coherence in an initiative, teachers gain a greater sense of how their goals fit into the overall goals of large-scale projects or initiatives.

Space and Resources to Support the Program

The provision of such technical resources as materials, time, and money is an important factor in the building of literacy-based school change. It is not so much an issue of volume of resources as it is determining what the appropriate resources are, based on the needs of your school. It is a matter of targeting needs and then finding resources that match those needs. Resources represent not only the materials that will be used, but also the professional development teachers will need to effectively teach literacy in their classrooms. Hence, time and money are as important as materials in implementing literacy initiatives.

Clearly, books are critical to literacy teaching, but the books that are chosen must match the needs of individual classes and students. This might be determined by such factors as whether a class has predominantly ESL/ELL students or whether there are more boys than girls in a classroom setting. It is particularly important to have a program in place that allows children to bring books home from school and perhaps have parents read to them.

Susan Schwartz highlights that an important part of a principal's job is ensuring that the teaching staff is equipped with what it needs to effectively teach literacy. This means taking account of macro-issues like program coherence and assessment alongside micro-issues like keeping tabs on the availability of supplies. She emphasizes:

> Resources are a large part of teaching, and teachers need to know that their
> resources are there for their programs.

What We Need to Observe in Our Literacy Schools

No one could have predicted the thousands of changes that have occurred in the teaching profession over the last thirty years in every English-speaking country. The authors of this book have been involved in writing curriculum guides and programs for five different governments through that time, and can't even count the educational thrusts we have experienced in the name of helping our youngsters learn — the institutes, workshops, seminars, speeches, in-service sessions, and courses we have attended. We have a wall of books and articles full of techniques, strategies, programs, and stories, chronicling our history in educational change. But one factor remains constant: every weekday morning, the students arrive at the school's doorstep, waiting (and even eager) to enter. We are heartened and strengthened by the continuing existence of the place we call school, and would like to celebrate those components of literacy that seem to have survived the years of turmoil, no matter what label we choose to describe our programs. We need to state up front that we have no fear of change; but how sweet it is to see in each new educational movement those teaching/learning events that remain significant staples of all powerful literacy classrooms.

Supporting All Students

We continue to help our students to experience what successful literacy events feel like, so they know they are supported in their struggle toward independence as readers and writers. We need to enlist their participation as they revalue their literacy selves, as we develop cooperatively a comprehensive and inclusive program for reading and writing. They need to make choices in their literacy lives, to sense ownership of their reading and writing selves, by selecting some of the books and resources they read, the topics they write about, and the projects they research. They care more about activities they feel they own, in which they want to invest their time and interest.

Students in difficulty need to experience what successful literacy events feel like, to know that there is hope for recovery, that they will be supported in their struggle to grow toward independence; they need to become readers and writers. Very few students are unable to master literacy; therefore, we need to recognize and help many different types of struggling readers and writers, to find out what they can do and build on their competencies, no matter how limited, so that they can move forward and recognize that they are indeed improving.

We make certain that learners with different strengths and challenges find themselves sitting alongside others in the classroom literacy community who are involved in and excited about learning, so that they have role models for what life in school could be, so that they can begin to sense how successful readers and writers function. We see older students become buddy readers with younger students, and watch as they began to see themselves as those who can read, who have power with print.

A sense of despair can inhibit or even prohibit literacy growth. There will be occasions when teachers will want to work with a small group of students who are having difficulties, but for the rest of the day, we need to make literacy events social and communicative experiences where readers of mixed abilities are interacting with satisfaction alongside their companions. Students having reading difficulties need to see themselves and to be seen by classmates as contributing members of the classroom community. During sharing times, they need to present to the class, and can do so with extra preparation and support. They need to show the books they have published, to present a book talk about a book they have read and enjoyed, to read a poem they have practiced, or to share excerpts from their journals. They can introduce or thank a speaker, review a film that they saw, or demonstrate an experiment with their group.

Most of all, students in literacy difficulty need to be recognized for their successes in the processes of reading and writing, to have their accomplishments celebrated. When they demonstrate growth or improvement, we can find ways to offer encouragement rather than public praise, to let them and others realize the distance they have traveled in literacy development.

Students who are struggling with their reading and writing have diverse needs and abilities. One published set of texts or series of remedial exercises just can't support alone the different approaches teachers need to use in designing programs for these students. Inappropriate instruction may delay or regress their growth.

What Does a Struggling Reader and Writer Look Like?

Some readers and writers in difficulty

- may not be involved in family literacy and seem unfamiliar with literature
- lack faith and confidence in the hope that they will learn to be effective readers and writers
- demonstrate frustration or apathy during reading times
- don't understand why reading can be worthwhile
- don't see technology, books, and other print resources as sources of pleasure and information
- need more time and experience with different forms of print
- avoid reading at every opportunity
- may not know the alphabet, or do not understand how print works in a text
- feel that reading is only the correct recognition and pronunciation of words
- don't know the basic rimes and sound/symbol patterns
- are unable to process new words as they read, and seldom reread to self-check and correct miscues
- have few strategies for dealing with unfamiliar words and over-rely on sounding out
- have difficulty matching their story-memory predictions with the actual print words
- are unable to recognize high-frequency words while reading
- seem to ignore punctuation that could increase comprehension
- do not read fluently, either silently or orally
- rely constantly upon the teacher for support in decoding and encoding words
- are unable to hold the parts of complex sentences in their minds to build the larger text meaning
- don't understand how a reader reads silently
- are afraid to take risks in order to construct meaning
- can't bring personal background information to meaning-making with a particular text
- can't repair a breakdown in meaning as they read
- focus on literal interpretation of text instead of inferring, analyzing, synthesizing, and extending the reading
- can't seem to monitor whether the reading experience makes sense
- are unable to predict future events in the text
- falter frequently while reading aloud, often pleading (even silently) for help
- cannot seem to retell a text
- don't understand how particular types of text, including digital texts, function
- are defeated by the length of the text
- can't seem to match their interests with any of the books in the classroom
- cannot select a book, or choose inappropriate books for their interests and abilities
- have not moved along in the stages of spelling
- don't understand where to find support for spelling difficult words
- have great difficulty with handwriting
- cannot find a topic to write about
- don't see a reasons for editing written work; never arrive at the publishing stage of writing
- are not growing in their use and knowledge of conventions in writing
- are unable to connect their own written expression with what they have read
- have difficulty participating in the social aspects of literacy
- seem unable to respond to the text in group discussions
- have difficulty in other subject areas that require literacy skills
- are unable to assess and reflect upon their literacy competence and experiences
- are learning to read and write in English as a second language, but are already literate in their home language

Students as Writers

We need to increase the time that students spend in writing, actually composing and arranging their ideas. For students in difficulty, talking about what they may write is a prerequisite for the process of writing, so that they are prepared and confident when they begin to compose their thoughts. Webs, lists, brainstormed ideas, and, of course, computers can help them to move immediately into the act of writing instead of worrying and stalling for time. They can innovate on the patterns and shapes of stories and poems that they have heard or read. Teachers can use the writing of other authors and of fellow students as models for exploring how writers work and how writing functions. We need to let the students in on the secrets of writing.

We need to take time to respond to their journals and letters as we encourage them to develop and expand their jottings and recollections. By doing so, we can redirect their reading, suggest new books, share our own writing journey, and elaborate upon their thoughts, so that they will be stimulated to continue their writing about reading.

Handwriting is a struggle for some students, leading to frustration and even withdrawal because they cannot represent their thoughts on paper in ways that promote an easy flow of ideas and communication to others. They are defeated by the mechanics. Authorities such as Donald Graves tell us that continuous writing through the years will support handwriting improvement, and that maturity will have an effect on how we form our words. Many students, especially boys, have been completely rescued by the computer, and now their handwriting has become legible and uniform because their confidence as communicators has blossomed.

Building Word Power

We especially need to build word power with readers and writers, so that they have an ever-increasing word bank of immediately recognizable words, effective ways to discover unknown words in their reading texts, and useful strategies for spelling words in their writing. They learn to notice how letters fit together, the patterns involved in word construction, how we can take words apart to discover their inner workings. We must remember that word power is cumulative and lifelong, and aim for significant individual growth from year to year.

We want students to become wordsmiths, to notice significant and special words, and to recognize words used effectively or in interesting ways, "ping-pong" words that sound delightful or funny, or words with unusual spellings.

Playful approaches and games may be our strongest allies. Computer programs are beginning to offer us intriguing ways for building word strength with spelling and vocabulary games and puzzles, as well as offering support for struggling handwriters and spellers. It is significant that many of the games onscreen offer openings to limited readers for taking part in print-based activities, with less frustration and defeat than in much paper-and-pencil work.

Guided Reading

We need to help students struggling with reading to learn the problem-solving strategies that proficient readers use to make sense of print experiences. Through explicit instructions during individual conferences and within guided reading time with a group of students, teachers can demonstrate how these effective

Regie Routman tells of a student who said that her first reading of the book was like a rough draft of her writing.

Many words that are recognized by students without our help occur because of impact rather than sequential teaching: names, brands, ads, heroes, and fast-food terms, to name a few. Margaret Phinney says, "They remember the meaningful, the outstanding and the useful first, and those are all determined by personal interest and purpose." How can we build on this knowledge base?

strategies work, and support students in their attempts to begin to incorporate them into their reading.

Daily guided reading periods should form the foundation of their reading program. Because these students require the most intensive and explicit teaching, small-group instruction using carefully selected texts and directed interaction should result in literacy progress that enables them to handle more difficult selections and books.

The choice of reading materials for guided reading may determine students' success as readers. We need to be certain that sets of books at appropriate reading levels are available for them to read. As well, we should look for the best books that we can find, so that the artistry of the author can help influence the competency of the reader. We need to focus on and make evident the reading strategies that help them to make meaning as they read, and this process requires success as a motivating force.

Too many challenges in a text may obstruct the literacy learning rather than move the child along. We want texts that enable youngsters to grow in their power with print, and that pique and maintain interest in continuing the selection. For example, the familiarity that develops with books in a series can help students ease into reading more and more texts, building on the momentum of what they already know, increasing fluency with automatically recognized vocabulary, patterns, author's style, and characters.

Concluding Thoughts

It is helpful and fruitful to look at product — *what* an effective school looks like; but it may be more useful to focus on process — *how* a school can become an improving school. To greater and lesser degrees, principal leadership, teacher knowledge and skills, a professional community, a literacy program, and technical resources already exist in all schools. It is now a matter of strengthening and sustaining these factors as girders for literacy-based school success that is based on solid research exploring different approaches to literacy development.

In the light of recent research studies, it is clear that principals who are working to develop knowledge and skills in their staffs are seeing changes in their teachers' attitudes towards teaching literacy. In turn, they are seeing changes in their students' attitudes and abilities in reading and writing — even in those with the challenges of a new country and a new language. The remaining challenge for most of these schools seems to be eliciting greater parental involvement in and parental support for literacy initiatives.

Ultimately, it is the personal satisfaction of becoming readers and writers that enables students to continue their efforts to become literate. Once a school leader ensures that the proper supports are in place for this to happen, success can be achieved in creating literacy-based school change.

Reflecting on the Literacy Program

- What are your own beliefs about helping children become readers and writers? How does your philosophy of literacy learning affect the programs in your school?
- What is your role as a professional development leader? How do you determine, organize, and implement professional development in your school community?
- How can the staff at your school take ownership of their professional development so that everyone wants to participate and it is significant for the school's overall literacy goals? What realities about the challenges faced by you and your teachers, and about possible changes that would make positive differences, do you need to share with regional/provincial leaders?
- What mechanisms does your school have in place for sharing and discussing books and articles of interest? How could these methods be made more effective?
- How can discussion on useful sources of information be more sufficiently focused? For example: Do teachers try out some of the good ideas found in these resources? Are there good sources of information that staff are overlooking?
- How can your school present its curriculum for literacy growth so that parents will understand the program and support the teachers? For example: Are there articles and books that could be made available to parents?
- What can your school do to include parents in a significant way in literacy initiatives?
- How can the school honor each family's way of life, while still developing a sense of school community? What changes might be necessary to promote multicultural awareness and respect for literacy development in all children?
- How can you include volunteers in the classroom to assist staff and students with various literacy activities? In what ways might parents, student teachers, high-school students, older student buddies, and invited guests contribute?
- What will be the benefits of volunteering for the volunteers, the teachers, the students, and your own work as an administrator?

Literacy-Based Change in Schools

Carol Rolheiser and Karen Edge

Dr. Carol Rolheiser is an associate dean at OISE/UT, as well as an authority on literacy-based school change, teacher change, and cooperative learning. She is the lead writer on three reports dealing with literacy-based school change at the district level. Karen Edge is a researcher and a co-writer of the reports.

Leadership

In our different research projects, we examine shared leadership, which does shift some of our thinking from the traditional roles of principal or vice-principal leadership within a school. In many of the initiatives where there is a literacy coordinator, we are examining how a shared leadership role for literacy works within the school.

Obviously, there are certain responsibilities that a principal has, such as greater accountability for certain aspects. However, literacy leaders can have other responsibilities. In this way, the staff views leadership around literacy as being a shared leadership role. The stronger the relationship between the roles of principal and literacy leader, the more impact it can have on the success of a literacy program. This is a true shift in our traditional ways of thinking about educational leadership. Shared leadership is not about assigning power to a role; rather, people assume a leadership role through their actions and because of their background experience. How these people engage with teachers, the status that the role assumes, the symbolism of that role and the respect for that role — these are really grounded in what they will bring to that role as individuals.

For example, we found many factors were connected with the success of literacy coordinators on literacy teams, such things as how able they were to bring a sense of not having their own agenda to the teachers, but an agenda based on their support of the identified needs of the teachers. Since they are interacting with teachers, they come to know what needs are being expressed, and they begin to muster their support conceptually, as opposed to saying, "We are doing big books, and I am going to come in and help you implement big books." Effective literacy coordinators have a stronger template of what might be valuable in supporting and urging people along the literacy continuum. Not only are they making connections to teachers' needs, but they also have a strong "teacher" sense of what might be helpful. They can feed that information in, using their own professional knowledge and practice to guide the learning process.

In our report on literacy-based change, we shared with staff from all the project schools what we viewed as super-accelerators — the things that really made a difference in literacy change in schools. The number-one accelerator was the literacy coordinator. We wanted to communicate the message, both at the district level and with policy makers, that this role has significant impact on literacy change in schools: an on-site person engaged in job-embedded professional learning for teachers; a resident authority.

Teachers' Knowledge, Skills, and Dispositions

You need to develop the school's capacity to have an impact on student achievement by keeping a clear focus on the quality of the teaching, of the literacy curriculum, of instruction, and of assessment. But in order to develop a school's capacity, you need to develop the teachers' knowledge, skills, and dispositions. The professional community calls this the Collaborative Work Environment.

This process allows teachers to work alongside one another, creating a culture of collaboration. As they look toward program coherence with a focus on literacy, that literacy focus acts as an integrator, helping teachers handle what is often felt as fragmented teaching duties and professional overload. In fact, as you are working toward program coherence within the area of literacy, other aspects in the school are being affected positively.

PROFESSIONAL DEVELOPMENT

Another super-accelerator for change involved opportunities for teacher cooperation within the school culture, for planning and working together, with literacy coordinators creatively advocating rescheduling to ensure that there was planning time. One school made that a priority — finding joint time for teachers to get together and plan and have professional learning opportunities. They generated the schedules and strategies that they needed for success. We are going to send these results out to all of the schools in our districts to share the wisdom that grows from participation: this is what teachers value and want.

Program Coherence

Educational change is not about starting with a restructuring mandate, where every school will have a literacy launch on such and such a date so that everybody can collaborate during that time. Rather, the staff members need to determine what they value, such as joint planning time, and from that, the desire grows to determine how that can come to fruition. We found that to build a creative curriculum requires a clear vision. You need to have your staff rallied around clear goals, and let your staff provide collaborative and collective leadership, with the teachers involved in making decisions on how they are going to focus their school change.

We worry that district and provincial or state procedures either bring coherence and/or work against it. For example, there can be a literacy coordinator in a school working well with the principal and having great effect. But if the district decides to eliminate the literacy coordinators for the next year, that will have a huge impact on school progress. That is why it is important to have across-school sharing, to create advocacy and to create awareness. That is why we are involved in educational research — to feed this information to the policy-makers.

The underlying principle for success appears to be related to program coherence. In whatever way schools choose to do it, they are saying: How do we make literacy learning happen from one grade to another? How do we ensure that teachers have a common language? Where do we put the budget for books — a library specifically for leveled reading? Teachers need to feel that they are investing in literacy. Making budget decisions for thousands of dollars represents visible support, and actually builds a cooperative work environment. All of this builds momentum as you engage a variety of stakeholders in literacy-based school change.

Technical Resources

Another significant factor is technical resources. Teachers need support in the case of literacy, such as having sets of leveled books. All of the successful schools we have observed have in common a strong curriculum and instruction focus, centred around good literacy initiatives and strong assessment programs. As leaders, you are building school capacity to enhance instructional quality to support student achievement.

Nine Areas of Content Knowledge
Children's Literacy Initiative

The participants in a conference organized by the Children's Literacy Initiative determined nine important categories of content knowledge that would be essential to principals in providing successful literacy instructional leadership.

1. School Culture

Principals need to understand the significance of entrenched philosophical and instructional habits that constitute a culture in a school — and his or her own power to change that culture. Every school has a culture, often referred to as "the way we do things around here." School change is rarely an easy task, but it is a goal worth struggling toward. The writings of organizational psychologist, Robert Evans (author of *The Human Side of School Change*) and Roland Barth, Director of the Principals' Center at Harvard, are good places to begin. Barth's work makes the case for the importance of collegiality, with an emphasis on trusting teachers to share leadership and creating an atmosphere where colleagues listen to one another. Shelley Harwayne has written persuasively about her successful experiences creating a community of learners, including students, teachers, and parents, who share a common vision in her 1999 book, *Going Public*.

2. What the Experts Say

Principals need to know the thinkers and practitioners in the field of literacy instruction who provide fresh ideas and useful models: researchers such as Dick Allington, author of *What Really Matters for Struggling Readers*; Pat Cunningham, author of *Phonics They Use*; Diane Snowball, a specialist on the teaching of spelling; and master practitioners such as Shelley Harwayne, Lucy Calkins, and Ralph Fletcher. These experts offer specific direction and practical advice on the best literacy instructional strategies. Principals need to read and reflect on the best-practices of these craft leaders and attend their presentations when possible.

3. Children's Literature

In order to create a community of readers, principals must actively read not only professional literature, but also quality children's literature. Principals should know a wide range of authors, genres, and sources of information about children's literature, such as *The Hornbook, The New Advocate*, the International Reading Association's yearly publication of *Children's Choices*, the children's literature web site, **www.carolhurst.com**, and School Library Journal's *Booklinks*. Principals should take every opportunity to share their love of books with their colleagues, faculties, parents, and students.

4. Current Instructional Models

As the primary filter for new programs, principals must be familiar with a wide range of current instructional models. Principals can take the lead by instituting collegial investigations that build capacity to understand the complexities of competing models. Principals have to help their teachers develop a high level of expertise in order to select the best approach for each individual student from a wide variety of choices, such as Reading Workshop, Balanced Literacy, explicit phonics, etc. Instructional leaders should also explore new, responsive models of education, such as writer's workshops that actively engage students in the experience of becoming authors. Good sources of information about instructional models can be found in the journal *Educational Leadership* and through attending national and regional conferences.

5. Curriculum

The challenge for a principal is to know his or her district's mandated curriculum and make sure teachers are able to deliver it. We define curriculum as content, materials, and means of assessment, regardless of the delivery system (see Instructional Models above). One group at the conference questioned the need for a prescribed curriculum, and the other group raised the question of who should make decisions about curriculum. Gerald Duffy's research shows that, the more standardized the curriculum, the lower the achievement rate. Inspiration for further exploration can be found in books such as Ernest Boyer's *The Basic School*, Joanne Hindley's *In the Company of Children*, *Lifetime Guarantees* by Shelley Harwayne, and *Understand by Design* by Grant Wiggins.

6. Learning Time and Space

As the key decision-maker for the use of time and space, principals must be aware of how the use of time and space affects instruction. Models such as literacy blocks, which give large chunks of uninterrupted time for instruction in reading and writing, have proven to be extremely useful. Teachers must have time for collegial professional development. The learning environment of classrooms and hallways should be organized by teachers in ways that maximize instruction and celebrate students' authentic work. Some sources to investigate are the work of researcher Lesley Mandel Morrow on the effects of the environment on students, CLI's website *Creating a Classroom Literacy Environment*, and Richard Allington's *What Really Matters for Struggling Readers*.

7. Assessment Practices

Principals need to know how best to use assessment data based on relevant content standards established with teachers, school communities, and parents. The focus of assessment should always be improving student learning. Teachers should always be assessing to monitor student progress and inform instruction. Principals can work to structure school schedules to provide ample opportunity for formative assessment (used by teachers during instruction) and for faculty meetings where student work can be discussed. Commercial products, such as Marie Clay's *An Observation Survey*, *ECLAS*, and the *Developmental Reading Assessment* are extremely helpful in ongoing assessment of student needs. The work of James Popham and *The Heart of the Matter* by Beverly Falk were mentioned.

8. Support for Struggling Students

Principals need to take a close look at how support is delivered to struggling students and how this support is organized. Most children in need of extra academic help should receive it from highly trained specialists in intense blocks of time. Principals must explore all the options for making this possible, such as using part of an after-school budget to support a reading specialist. Other innovative solutions can be achieved through the use of learning support teams, parent–teacher coalitions, and summer school programs. Recent research has demonstrated that not all interventions are helpful. Allington's *What Really Matters for Struggling Readers* is a concise summary of how to transform recent research findings into practical solutions.

9. Research

Principals need to know where to find models, data, and organizations that do useful research and that can serve as allies in answering questions of what works and why. The *Eric Clearinghouse on Reading, English and Communication* at **www.indiana.edu/~eric_rec** is an excellent source for literacy research updates, with links to the web pages of the Center for Improvement of Early Reading Achievement (CIERA), the Center on English Learning and Achievement (CELA), and the National Reading Panel, among others. At the website of the International Reading Association (IRA) at **www.reading.org**, *Reading Research Quarterly*, the world's leading literacy research journal, is available online. The Laboratory for Student Success (LSS) is the Regional Educational Laboratory that focuses on educational leadership; a variety of research resources on educational reform and urban education can be found on its website at **www.temple.edu/lss**. *Strategies*, published by Panasonic Foundation and The American Association of School Administrators, can be found online at **www.aasa.org/publications/strategies/index.htm**. Using such resources can provide direction through the maze of information now available.

Enrique A. Puig is the Director of the Florida Literacy and Reading Excellence Center at the University of Central Florida. In addition to being president of the Orange County Reading Council (Florida), Enrique serves as an elected board member of the American Reading Forum and continues to work with students.

Kathy S. Froelich has provided professional development opportunities to teachers and literacy coaches at the national level. She is currently teaching at Florida State University.

The Literacy Coach
Enrique A. Puig and Kathy S. Froelich

Visualize a traditional arch. The keystone at the top of the arch prevents it from collapsing. At the base of the arch are cornerstones, supporting and sustaining it. Based on experience and research, we can see the principal as the keystone that supports the overarching issue of effective literacy instruction in school (Booth & Rowsell, 2002). The literacy leadership team, supported and guided by a knowledgeable literacy coach, are two of the cornerstones needed to sustain and expand effective literacy instruction (Puig & Froelich, 2007). Implementing this system of support will propel learning and teaching forward.

Remove either the keystone or the cornerstones, and more than likely the arch will fall. The same principle of architectural design applies to any school reform model that does not work toward building a school where everyone is learning

(Tharp & Gallimore, 1988). Although it is critical for the principal to be a literacy leader and a "lead learner," a literacy leadership team and the literacy coach who guides it are crucial to promoting forward shifts in literacy instruction and learning (Booth & Rowsell, 2002). As a result, an effective literacy leader not only takes into account the formation of a diverse literacy leadership team, but also includes the implementation and utilization of a people-friendly, knowledgeable literacy coach (Puig & Froelich, 2007).

Four elements represent the four cornerstones that should be in place for forward shifts to occur in schools:

- a well-researched and designed K–12 literacy framework of instructional practices that includes parents and community to support implementation for classroom teachers
- the literacy leadership team
- an established assessment program (static and dynamic)
- the literacy coach

A well-designed K–12 literacy framework of instructional practices provides classroom teachers with critical information regarding what routines and rituals students use, and what rituals and routines students need to be prepared for in the future. Think of K–12 instructional practices as the crystal ball that provides teachers a glimpse into students' instructional pasts and futures, information they use to support the implementation of powerful and relevant lessons that amplify instruction for students to promote acceleration in learning (Bodrova & Leong, 1996).

At the elementary level (pre-K–Grade 5), the literacy leadership team is a ménage that consists of the principal (always), the literacy coach (again, always), one teacher representative from each grade level, a media specialist, other special area teachers (e.g., art, music, physical education), and a parent representative. At the secondary level (Grades 6–12), the literacy leadership team is similar in that the principal and the literacy coach are members; however, the makeup of classroom teacher membership differs: each content area (language arts, mathematics, science, social studies, vocational education, etc.) is represented by a teacher, rather than having a teacher from each grade level. At any level, the strength of the team is dependent on the mélange of experiences and beliefs of the members.

The role of the literacy leadership team is to collaboratively investigate and address learning and teaching issues in order to improve instructional practices and student learning simultaneously. In effect, the team is ethnographic in nature — one that studies the strengths and needs of a school by collecting artifacts, using participant and non-participant observations to make powerful and relevant decisions. The team generally goes through a mental framework of ascertaining an initial theme of significance (identifying strengths and needs), further scrutinizing the designated theme of significance, drafting a blueprint of support, executing the design of support, and reflecting on the construction and implementation of the design after execution.

The first task of the literacy team is to ascertain an initial significant theme to scrutinize further. This may demand reviewing static and dynamic assessments, along with student/teacher interviews, so that the team can arrive at the core of the significant theme. A full investigation of assessment will give the team a truer picture of the source of the concern or theme of significance than reliance on just one type of assessment can obtain. If there is no in-depth examination, it may cause misinterpretation of the problem investigated (Dixon-Krauss, 1996). By and large, static data provide educators with a score and compare large groups to other large groups to form a generalized theme of significance to investigate further; for example, many US states and Canadian provinces have implemented a state- or province-wide test to be administered, usually in fourth, eighth, and tenth grades. In the best situations, state-wide tests serve as gauges to indicate how students, classes, schools, school systems, and states are doing in comparison to other students, classes, schools, school systems, and states. Does static assessment provide useful information? Yes. Does static assessment provide the classroom teacher with the necessary information to guide appropriate instruction? No. Does static assessment provide a literacy leadership team critical information to effectively problem-solve? Not quite.

When coupled with dynamic assessment, however, static assessment not only has the potential to address the surface structures of a theme or concern, but also can spearhead and guide the team to consider the deep structures of a theme or concern. Dynamic assessment supports principals, literacy leadership teams, and classroom teachers in looking at how students are processing information, so that the classroom teacher can implement efficient and effective instructional practices that scaffold students' journeys toward flexible and independent learning. Some examples of dynamic assessments are informal reading inventories, running records, performance assessments, student portfolios, and student writing samples. Experienced classroom teachers, principals, and literacy leadership teams take these assessment tools and more into account to dig deeper when investigating a theme of significance.

The utilization of a literacy coach buttresses all literacy leadership team endeavors. The role of a literacy coach has many facets on a continuum of professional development (Puig & Froelich, 2007). The literacy coach serves as the conduit of information between the principal, the team, the teachers, and the community, to not only ensure a common language, but also to maintain up-to-date research and instructional practices (Puig & Froelich, 2007). Since language is a tool for thinking (Vygotsky, 1992), developing and updating a common language is critical for the team. It falls on the literacy coach's shoulders to support, encourage, and challenge (respectfully and sensitively) the principal, team members, teachers, and community members. When the literacy coach ensures that all involved have a clear understanding of literacy as a process, there is less chance that data can be misinterpreted and lead a school in the wrong direction. Clay (2001) tells us that, unless teachers have a clear understanding of literacy as a process, their teaching will be hit or miss. Likewise, if a literacy leadership team does not understand literacy as a process, ascertaining an initial theme of significance and scrutinizing it will be hit or miss.

In a school reform system, the principal as a lead learner, a literacy coach, teachers, and community members are powerful components that can bring about forward shifts in learning and teaching; without real experiences in which the members of the team engage with students, it is all theory on paper. We strongly believe that, in order to execute any school reform success — for real change to take place, sustain, and expand — every member interested in improving learning and teaching needs to be working with students in a consistent and practical manner. In other words, principals, literacy coaches, parents, and community members (and, of course, teachers) need to be working with students. They have to come to the table with relevant participant observations based on real work with real students. Only then can data be triangulated with artifacts and non-participant observations, the ultimate goal for all literacy leadership teams.

Being a Literacy Coach
Lea Pelletier

Lea Pelletier has been a classroom teacher, resource teacher, and administrator at both elementary and secondary levels. She is a senior-high literacy coach for two rural high schools in Nova Scotia.

Two years ago, when I was asked to take one of two new positions in our province as a senior high literacy coach, I was intrigued. After a variety of experiences in education — teaching, administrating, and consulting — I had chosen to return to the classroom, and had been there for two years. I was very happy where I was, but this offer sounded like a wonderful learning experience, and it would mean another full-time position for my school; it was impossible to decline.

From the very first, I was strongly supported by people who had great gifts to give. Our English Language Arts Consultant at the Department of Education gave moral support, supplied hundreds of professional and student resources, and organized regular professional development and meetings with other coaches in the province. The Literacy Coordinator at our school board provided a great professional support, a laptop, and many other practical resources that made it easy for me to work.

As I read in preparation over that first summer, it became clear quite quickly that, although there are some characteristics common to all coaching, some aspects may differ from one area or site to another. I thought a great deal about the teachers in my school, and met with my principal to discuss what coaching might look like here. She was very supportive and encouraged keeping it flexible, defining the position by what teachers would identify as their needs and concerns. She also spread word of the position and, three weeks before school even began in the fall, I was already coaching a few teachers who were going to be teaching courses that were new to them. This is a small rural school, so it is common for teachers to have assignments that include six or more separate preparations, some of which are not in the curriculum areas for which they trained.

On the first day of school, I was given time in the staff meeting to introduce my new position and to invite teachers to work with me. Using an idea from one of the books I had read, I said that when considering how I might be able to help them, they should think of the "burrs under their saddles," the situations in which their expectations of students' literacy in their courses were not being met.

Involvement with Teachers

One of the practical issues we faced was that there was no room in the school for me to have an office. It might have been possible for me to move from classroom to classroom when teachers had work periods, but that would make it difficult for others to find me when they wanted to talk. We decided, instead, to make a corner for me in the staffroom. At first this seemed awkward and problematic, but it turned out to be an unexpected blessing. It meant that I was always present at recess and lunch breaks, joining in on conversations as a member of staff but also listening for professional needs and concerns. It also meant that if a teacher came into the staffroom after a particularly difficult class, I was there and ready to talk at the perfect time. Any concerns I had had about lack of privacy as I coached a teacher were soon allayed. If a conversation I was having needed to be confidential, we could always find a small private space somewhere; but mostly, teachers were happy to work with me even if others could hear us. Often a teacher working nearby would join in on our conversation, either to gain information or to offer suggestions. Over a period of months in the first year, the staffroom culture became noticeably more collegial, positive, and learning-centred. This experience stressed how important being available during free time can be to success in coaching.

My collaborations with teachers have come about in many different ways:

- through staffroom conversations
- because another staff member suggested a teacher talk with me
- because a teacher wanted specific information or materials
- because a teacher wanted to solve a problem with a particular lesson or unit

Usually, our work together has begun with something fairly small — looking for a pre-reading activity for a particular class, looking for an article to support a lesson — and built from there. Small successes have led to larger questions. Teachers have been wonderful about using their work periods to see me, but we have also been generously supported by both the Department of Education and the school principal, who have arranged for teachers to have substitutes for day-long coaching sessions when needed. It is during these days that the most important individual professional development has taken place. Time has allowed us to spread out materials and assess their value, to tackle the "big picture" issues, to build visions together, to form the personal and professional bonds that build trust, to make the first steps toward large leaps in professional practice.

As teachers have come to work with me, my job description has grown to include helping with anything that would assist them in supporting students' literacy:

- sharing comprehension activities and organizers
- pre-digesting and sharing the best professional resources, either by talking about them or by copying short, useful sections
- observing and helping with classroom management issues
- helping to plan literacy lessons
- helping to plan units with balanced approaches to literacy
- helping to plan whole courses so that literacy practices are embedded
- helping to plan a cross-curricular literacy-based approach to a science fair
- devising and producing forms and organizers to support lessons, units, and courses
- locating helpful teaching resources and getting permission to purchase them
- locating supplementary and alternative text for students
- locating experienced teachers in content areas, and arranging for new teachers to visit with them
- co-teaching literacy activities in the classroom
- training teachers to administer and grade baseline literacy assessments
- reporting on the results of baseline assessments
- facilitating subject-area committees

- helping to establish a cross-curricular site-based team to coordinate support for students with literacy needs

Working with Administration

The principal's initial openness to my work has only grown. In the first year, she agreed to focus all site-based professional development on literacy. In one of two staff meetings each month, I was able to involve teachers in activities that support comprehension strategies. As well, in several half-day or full-day sessions, we introduced the language of literacy to the whole staff. She also asked me to write a monthly column in the school newsletter, so that parents and guardians could be included in what we were learning. In the second year, we continued the staff-meeting professional development as it was, but took our guidance on longer sessions from the teachers; we listened for "hot topics" involving literacy, and I designed sessions around them. It has been wonderful to see how these sessions, responding to teachers' own concerns about their students, have built a sense of team and mission.

Over the course of the first year, the principal and I talked many times about how the school might best support students' literacy at the senior-high level. We considered Learning Strategies courses, and Grade 10 courses in language arts and mathematics that would allow students to get two credits in each by taking them every day through the year. In a small school, introducing these courses would mean a major overhaul to the school timetable, but the principal embraced the change. Together, we talked through the whole process and developed a radically different timetable with literacy support at its core. She has much of which to be proud, and the students are benefiting.

Challenges in High-School Literacy

In working as a literacy coach, I have become very familiar with a number of challenges to establishing a comprehensive literacy approach at the high-school level. The first is the need to know your students as individual readers and writers. This becomes tricky when a teacher may see 100–180 students in the course of a day. At our small school, it is not a major problem — teachers often know not only the students but also the parents well — but even here we have found the development of a site-based team, which discusses the needs of all students in the school and then coordinates the available support, to be extremely helpful in sharing information about the literacy needs of our students. The inclusion of Learning Strategies courses has also helped, as teachers of those courses are in close contact with their students' other teachers, sharing information about literacy needs and successes.

A second challenge has been the concern of high-school content area teachers that taking time for literacy activities will keep them from helping their students to meet course outcomes, and their sense that literacy is one more thing added onto their already full plates. I have been careful to stress that no one expects a content area teacher to show students how to decode. Rather, they are the experts on how to read and write successfully in their subject areas, and so must be the ones to share those secrets with their students, so that the students can use their course-specific literacy to achieve the outcomes. One helpful approach has been to show teachers how much of the language of literacy is embedded in the curriculum guides, and how many of the content outcomes assume literacy.

Another approach has been to demonstrate, through cooperative planning, how a lesson can be constructed so that students are learning the content at the same time as they are developing their literacy skills.

A third major challenge at high schools is the physical thickness, and the density and difficulty of the language, of many high-school textbooks. Much of my work with teachers has involved guiding them to use the gradual-release-of-responsibility approach to teach students how to make meaning from these books. As well, we have discussed the idea that, while textbooks can be wonderful supports for teaching a curriculum, they are not the curriculum; teachers are free to use other text materials that will help students to meet their outcomes. This discussion, followed by help in finding more engaging and accessible texts, has brought some great successes in the classroom. Teachers who struggled with units that students found boring and difficult now talk about how much more engaged and successful students are.

What I Have Learned

TO ASK RATHER THAN TELL, AND LISTEN RATHER THAN TALK

In coaching individual teachers, I have found that the two most important skills are questioning and active listening. Quite often, the request which brings a teacher to me has little to do with the deeper issues that he or she wants addressed, so I am careful to "listen between the lines." It is also important not to jump in and "fix" a problem until teachers have discovered the solutions themselves; thoughtful questioning and active listening allow me to suggest many possible paths without choosing for them the ones they will take.

TO HAVE COMPASSION

Coaching allows you to get close to colleagues, to see through their eyes and understand their feelings. Once you have been that close, it becomes impossible to judge.

TO BE PATIENT

Not every teacher feels ready to be coached. Some will take time, and others may never come. All a coach can do is to invite a few times, smile and keep the doors open.

From Student Response to Effective Literacy Teaching
Jeannie Wilson

"Jeannie, can you do an in-service on effective literacy assessment at our staff meeting next Monday?"

"My teachers are struggling with time. How do they take the time required for literacy and still cover the curriculum?"

"What does balanced literacy look like in an intermediate classroom?"

"I have subject specialists who don't see literacy as their responsibility."

Jeannie Wilson is a Literacy Resource Teacher with the Simcoe County District School Board. There, she extends the work of her doctoral dissertation, which examined the relationship between teacher development and teaching practices in adolescent literacy.

"Can you work with us on data analysis and goal-setting to improve student achievement?"

"Help!"

Literacy has been the focus of my teaching and learning for the past eight years, most recently as an Itinerant Literacy Resource Teacher K–12, serving 41 schools. In all the turmoil of changing roles, supporting the implementation of provincial, board, and school priorities, and working alongside a breathtakingly diverse array of teachers, one thing has remained constant: what works for our students as literacy learners works for us as literacy teachers.

Colleagues and I have surveyed several thousand Simcoe County students over the past few years, asking them two questions: "If you could teach teachers *one thing* about teaching you reading, what would it be? If you could teach teachers *one thing* about teaching you writing, what would it be?" Students' responses guide my work with their teachers.

"Give Us Choice"

Teaching teachers is a challenge! Understanding where they are in their literacy perspectives and practices is essential if we are to become a true learning community. Whenever possible, I start our work with a professional version of the literacy survey: "What is the greatest literacy need of the students you teach? What is *your* greatest need as a literacy teacher?" Providing this opportunity yields rich insights, particularly with secondary colleagues who don't think of themselves as literacy teachers:

> I come from a place where I didn't know much or think much about literacy because I'm literate, highly literate by most standards. I assumed that everybody had some sort of proficiency that was on the same spectrum as mine, maybe just not with as many years of experience. I've realized that just isn't true. Things [related to reading and writing] that I know innately, these kids haven't got a clue about, some of the ones I teach. It becomes a problem: how do I get them to get their feet on the first rung of the ladder?

When teachers' individual voices are included in the learning conversation from the outset, when their specific needs are an integral part of what we do and how we do it, we create the conditions where teacher growth can have an immediate impact on student achievement. Regie Routman agrees:

> … all learning involves conversation. … That conversation may be with ourselves, between ourselves and an author's words on the page, with a colleague, with a mentor, with an apprentice, with a student. … We teachers need to initiate and participate in the conversations that must take place for "best practice" to flourish and for our students to thrive.

"Make Learning Relevant"

Important as it is, purposeful talk about literacy teaching and learning is not enough. Learning communities need to become communities of practice

(Wenger, 1998). Consider this teacher's response to Cris Tovani's book *I Read It, But I Don't Get It: Comprehension Strategies for Adolescent Readers*:

> Tovani talks about the class full of deadpan faces [with] no curiosity. I have felt that a lot too. The one thing I like about this profession is dealing with kids who are so full of energy and curiosity and I've questioned myself sometimes if I could actually continue with the job. Sometimes I walk into a class and they just sit there and there is just no burning light in them. There is no curiosity and they start to suck the energy out of me. You know the force they have. I'm staring at them thinking, "I have zero energy now. Thanks."

When this teacher spoke, every one of his peers nodded knowingly. Motivating adolescent learners is a common dilemma. My job is to move us beyond stories that articulate this struggle to classroom practices that address it constructively. Relevant teacher development makes student work the basis for our growth.

We have our students write a personal essay on "The True Meaning of ..." something that is important to them. We each write one first and share it with our classes. We provide a student exemplar. We suggest possible topics to those who want them: school, friends, music, family, sports. The work students produce focuses our future work — with them, first and foremost; then with one another as we hone our craft.

Relevant literacy teaching and learning isn't always this straightforward. Teachers who do not teach language or English find it hard to relate to Randy Bomer's approach:

> I ... prefer to block at the door anything that does not contribute directly to my main objective in literacy teaching—supporting students in making meaning of the lives they live and crafting those meanings for authentic purposes (1995).

For cross-curricular literacy support, I turn to teachers themselves. We identify a specific literacy skill students require for a particular unit. We choose an appropriate strategy to develop this skill, drawing from resources like the curriculum-specific "Think Literacy" documents. We seek several texts that address the unit content in diverse ways. Ideally, we meet with others teaching the same course before, during, and after the unit to share our practices, analyze student work, and determine next steps. In my experience, teachers who do this find that their classrooms are more like Bomer's than they thought, as students experience greater success in making meaning and connecting their learning in mathematics, history, and science to their lives outside the classroom.

"Don't Just Tell; Show"

When I reflect on my years in the classroom, I am chastened by the realization of how often I abandoned effective teaching practice: *I do / You watch; I do / You help; You do / I help; You do / I watch* (Wilhelm, Baker & Dube, 2001). In our rush to cover the curriculum, many teachers resort to *I tell / You do*. It doesn't work with our students and it doesn't work with us.

In the best of all possible worlds, teachers of many subjects and grades form a community of practice to improve literacy teaching and learning. This community may begin as a book study, a provincial or board-funded learning team, or an Additional Qualifications course. Over time, as trust builds and understanding deepens, we open our practice to our peers — not "This is what I did, and this is what happened" but "Here is my lesson, and here is the student work. I'm celebrating this and I'm struggling with this." In the best of all possible worlds, teachers are working on a common literacy need, applying the same strategies in diverse contexts. The learning that ensues is transformational.

What if leaders don't have the wherewithal to create such communities? In Simcoe County, we have turned to Demonstration Classrooms with powerful results. Up to five teachers from a school spend a day living literacy from the inside out:

- 100 minutes: classroom observation
- 100 minutes: discussion with the classroom master teacher
- 100 minutes: application and planning with the literacy resource teacher

This is the real world of every classroom: split grades, eleven students on Individual Education Plans, interruptions, eruptions. It is the real world of the effective classroom: structure, balance, growth, consistency, hilarity, and always, always literacy.

Change takes time. Teachers tell and show us it is time well spent:

In all I do I strive to consider the importance of the "big picture" and that has helped me to defend literacy to some of my students. I need to be more aware of what can work to help my students buy into their learning. If I can only help them understand that literacy will define who they are, maybe they will stop resisting.

I was great at entertaining kids, doing things that were fun and engaging. I knew that students enjoyed my classes but I really wasn't convinced that their skill levels, what they could actually do and produce were any different when they left my classroom. … [Now I know] the importance of repeating, repeating, repeating. On the wall of my classroom I have a big chart explaining how to make your thinking visible. I give them some sentence starters. I've modeled it first.

I've learned how to figure out the areas of the reading task that the student might be having difficulty with. I'm looking more at the skills the student is able to demonstrate or practice. It's finding ideas that are implied and making connections that are difficult. I'm getting a sense of how to go ahead.

Building Effective Mentoring Relationships
Jim Strachan

Jim Strachan is the Program Coordinator working with beginning teachers for the Toronto District School Board. He writes about and gives workshops on the role of mentoring in teacher development.

A beginning teacher walks into a school for the first time…. What are the initial and ongoing structures that will allow of the "intentional" sharing of knowledge and practice?

This question has been at the heart of our work with beginning teachers and mentors in the Toronto District School Board for the last three years. Throughout this work, the importance of school culture is a recurring theme. Simply put, the support of the principal, teachers, and other staff members at school plays a defining role in the experiences of beginning teachers.

By employing multiple models of mentoring based on the needs of their beginning teachers, administrators can facilitate job-embedded opportunities for professional growth for all staff. Below are some specific examples of the differentiation that can occur in mentoring at the school level.

Multiple Models of Mentoring

Multiple models of mentoring can co-exist in the same school/site, often to the benefit of the protégé.

BROKER MENTOR	
Role	• Mentor provides orientation to school logistics and culture • Mentor brokers involvement of colleagues as needs arise from protégé
Considerations	• Consultant-type relationship, fewer opportunities for collaboration and coaching • May be initial support until other mentoring relationships are established or ongoing throughout the year
ONE-TO-ONE MENTOR MATCHING	
Role	• Mentor is site-based and is matched on an individual basis with a protégé • Mentor adopts consultant, collaboration, and coaching stances based on the needs of the protégé
Considerations	• Mentor/protégé relationships that flourish are reciprocal — both parties learn and grow • Greater "ownership" if the mentor has volunteered and if protégé has been involved in the determination of which person will be the mentor
GROUP MENTORING	
Role	• Mentor works with two or more protégés; or protégé may have two or more mentors • School mentoring committee plans formal support and professional learning opportunities for both mentors and protégés
Considerations	• Provides flexibility if school has large number of beginning teachers (or mentors) • This model is often embedded in a school-wide "mentoring culture" where all staff are mentors or protégés (or both)
INFORMAL MENTORING	
Role	• Protégé informally connects with a variety of staff members as needs arise • Mentor/protégé roles are fluid — often referred to as peer mentoring as, in many cases, the informal mentors are beginning teachers themselves
Considerations	• Spontaneous, informal nature of relationship can lend itself to collaboration • Protégé may feel isolated and/or disconnected if not part of any informal relationships
ONLINE MENTORING	
Role	• Using online conferences, protégés can participate in discussion and sharing with both experienced teachers and other beginning teachers
Considerations	• Enables access to a variety of resources and perspectives beyond the school site • Not all protégés feel comfortable sharing issues and concerns in this public a forum

Getting Started: Some Ideas to Consider

As administrators interacting with beginning teachers, we might consider a few guiding principles as we move forward to build instructional excellence in our classrooms.

THE HEART AND THE ART OF TEACHING AND LEARNING

Looking at what beginning teachers report as their issues and challenges, we see their concern is more "how to teach" than a desire for content knowledge of curriculum. The "what to teach" will come in time, but the how must be in place for learning to occur. Building inclusion in the classroom, meeting diverse learning needs, and assessing and evaluating student work in a meaningful manner are the key areas cited by beginning teachers. Both the formal and informal professional learning opportunities and supports that we offer at the school level must align with these key areas of need.

POWER AND DANGER OF THE ANECDOTE

Everybody in education has a story about being a first-year teacher. These anecdotes represent powerful entry points into this work, but they come with a caveat. In our desire to help, we often offer advice to beginning teachers based on our personal experiences and, while this advice is often well-meaning, it may not apply to each individual. Related to this is the idea of differentiation in the professional learning opportunities we offer beginning teachers. A "layered" design featuring multiple models of school-based mentoring, local coaching support, and online conferencing is more likely than a one-size-fits-all approach to meet the diverse learning styles and learning needs of our beginning teachers.

ATTRIBUTES-BASED APPROACH

Our beginning teachers collectively bring a tremendous array of previous life experiences and learning to their new role. In many cases, they bring energy, enthusiasm, and an ability to form authentic connections with students to our schools. If we believe our beginning teachers possess strengths and attributes, then we will structure opportunities for them to learn, from and with each other, instead of taking a "deficit" approach that implies our role is to fill them up with our personal knowledge.

SCHOOL IS WHERE THE LEARNING OCCURS

It is here that we have come full circle. By embedding formal and informal learning opportunities into the daily experiences of our beginning teachers, we will be giving both our teachers and our students a tremendous gift. Our students will be in the classrooms of teachers who are not only provided with resources, but are also part of a learning community where challenge is created and professional vision is encouraged.

By providing ongoing consulting, collaborating, and coaching opportunities for our mentors and beginning teachers, we will in effect model the very learning community we would like beginning teachers to create and promote in their own classrooms.

CHAPTER 2

Understanding Literacy Principles and Practices

Reading about complex public issues like climate change is not for the faint of heart. In addition to what we normally think about the nature of reading we — all of us — need to read into the use of words and images, in text, in talk, in tables, charts, and graphs. What may be reported as a fact may, in fact, be an opinion supported or not supported by evidence. How do we know? More reading, of course: deeper, more varied, with a major dose of thinking in the mix.

John Myers, Curriculum Instructor, Teacher Education Program, OISE

What We Know about Literacy

See Leading for Literacy: Roles of the Leader by Kathryn Broad on page 70.

Changes taking place within the field of literacy education do not entirely result from theoretical or methodological shifts, but also from shifts in the pedagogical infrastructure of elementary schooling. As we discussed in Chapter 1, the shifting administrative paradigm directly affects how your staff teaches literacy and your students learn to be literate. However, it is also necessary to consider: What will be the base upon which you can place your new role and responsibilities?

In deciding what needs to be taught and how it should be taught to encourage literacy growth, it is important to consider questions such as

- What is currently known about literacy teaching and learning?
- How do we define "reading"?
- How do people learn to read?
- What is decoding?
- What is phonics?
- What is reader response?
- How do teachers accommodate for special-needs students in early reading?
- How do people learn to write?
- What components are necessary for an effective literacy program?
- How important is technology in literacy learning?
- How can principals work with colleagues and parents to create an optimum literacy environment for students?

Certain lasting beliefs and understandings underpin effective literacy teaching and learning.

- Every child can learn to read and write, given time and support.
- High expectations are fundamental for all staff and students.
- Schools and classes are organized to reflect a commitment to maximizing student learning time.

- Learning to read and write are processes brought to life by effective literacy teaching.
- Each staff member makes a difference.
- Professional learning is an ongoing and essential aspect of continuous improvement.
- A whole-school and community approach involving students, teachers, parents, and the community consolidates student learning.
- Working in collaboration with families not only strengthens the nexus between school and home, but also offers additional opportunities to promote high expectations.
- Student performance is significantly influenced by teachers' standards and expectations.
- Every learner is different and we should use whatever means and methods we have at hand to facilitate student learning and achievement.

In this chapter, we set out to consolidate an understanding of the principles and practices upon which successful literacy initiatives can be based if everyone is committed to the process of literacy-based school change.

Thinking Outside the Box: The New Literacies

As a literacy principal, you guide the culture of the school. Committed to literacy, you create capacity in your school for making a real difference for students. Making a difference sometimes means thinking outside the box and creating space for innovation. Innovation can entail letting in influences from outside of school, such as different cultures, new media, digital and print technologies, and texts that exist in student's outside worlds.

See Play and Literacy by Linda Cameron on page 72.

New Texts, New Skills

Literacy has changed so much over the past decade that there is often a disconnect between what our students are doing outside of school walls and the work they are doing inside of school. Although we want our students to be proficient readers and writers of traditional texts, we need to be aware of and understand the kinds of texts that they appreciate and that garner their interest. By bridging a gap between their interests and school literacy, we are meeting them halfway and harnessing practice to their literacy strengths. See page 46 for is a list of non-traditional texts alongside skills that they carry or imply when you teach them to students.

New texts feature prominently in students' outside worlds. In understanding them, you meet your students halfway.

New Texts	Skills
Blogs	• Reflective free writing • Visuals used to say what words cannot • Intertextuality: tying disparate texts within a single one • Awareness of linked texts (i.e., hyperlinks) • Expressing identity through words, pictures, illustrations, and animation
Texting	• Understanding abridged text • Use of and proficiency with codes • Recognizing unofficial voice and register vs. more official voice and register • An understanding that texting is appropriate in some contexts (outside of school and at home) and not in other contexts (during school time)
Magazines	• Sense of genre (e.g., *Teen People* vs. car or computer magazines) • Understanding use of headings as index for content • Reading metaphors and messages in photographs • Use of figurative language in journalistic writing • Perceiving stereotypes and underlying messages in magazine photographs • Sensitivity to visual communication of layout
Television	• Understanding of characterization • Sense of genre (e.g., sitcoms vs. reality shows) • Reading gesture, movement onscreen • Recognizing affective speech (e.g., serious, comedic)
Video Games	• Problem-solving • Understanding identity formation • Evaluating settings and movements in settings • Advanced vocabulary • Social interaction through chatrooms and voice-activated speech
Game Cards	• Advanced vocabulary • Understanding characterization and complex story lines • Interpersonal practices with cards • Intertextuality: seeing a relationship between cards, websites, and television shows based on the same story line (e.g., Pokemon, Naruto)
Movies	• Understanding of voice and figures of speech • Understanding characterization, plot, and story line • Intertextuality: ties to books and games (e.g., *Cars, Shrek*) • Awareness of semiotic elements of film (e.g., close-ups vs. landscape camera shots)
Family Artifacts	• Use as expressions of identity • Valuing practices that artifacts might carry with them • Artifacts from home can tell you a great deal about the learner – their motivation and what they value • Tie to different cultures and languages
Zines	• Expressive writing about keen interests • Understanding of journalistic voice • Use of visuals to express words • Taking a position on an issue and making a statement about it • Technological ability: creating HTML code and hyperlinks to related texts
Cartoons and Comics	• Understanding of characterization and how it shifts in different contexts • Use of figures of speech • Use of visuals to create affect • Awareness of nuances of speech (e.g., sarcasm) • Perceiving what comics and cartoons teach about life
Music	• Poetic speech • Expressing identity and life events in music • Creating videos from songs • Connecting culture and music (e.g., reggae and Jamaican culture)

Although we have looked at just a sample of the texts within the communication landscape, we see a great complexity of thought and understanding in our students' interests and outside-school practices. Each genre of new texts tell us three valuable things about our students and what drives their worlds:

- They need and want to tie literacy to their identity.
- Different genres of texts carry skills that we need to harness to our teaching.
- Students have a tacit understanding of many of the concepts that we teach at school—such as comprehending story lines, settings, and characterization—from different genres of texts.

Manga, for instance, carries with it complex story lines, definitive characters, advanced vocabulary, complex contexts, and some comprehension of cultural nuances in texts such as *Naruto*.

Picture of a Learner: Rob and Naruto

Jennifer Rowsell

Rob (a pseudonym) is a special-education student at a suburban high school in New Jersey. Rob struggles with his literacy much of the time, yet he cannot get enough of Naruto. Naruto is an *anime* and *manga* series created by Masashi Kishimoto that depicts the life of a loud, hyperactive, young ninja with the great aspiration of becoming a Hokage. The story combines the long history of the ninja with levels of power and prestige based on *chakra*, the points of power, wisdom, and strength that we channel through our mind, body, and spirit. I learned all of this from Rob when I interviewed him in his school's computer lab for a study, which looks at reading practices online, that I am conducting with Anne Burke. Rob is a loner and occupies much of his time with *manga* texts, cards, and games that are tied to such series as Naruto and Yu-Gi-Oh. Rob is articulate and passionate about his love of *manga*, yet he has trouble with his reading and writing at school. Here is a sample of my conversation with Rob about the plot of Naruto.

ROB: This was in a recent episode that only comes out on Saturdays. They show last week's episode and then a new episode. Well, this one was still kind of recent at the Chuunin exams right after the preliminary rounds (Rob points to a character). That's Saski. He's in pretty bad shape. (We read text together, *Takoshi reaches Saski's hospital room just in time to stop Kuboto. His cover being blown, Kuboto answers Takoshi's question scornfully.*) What does scornful mean?
JENNIFER: Like resentfully or reprimanding.
(Rob reads more text and then asks about the word "inevitable.")
JENNIFER: Means destined to happen or it's going to happen.

You can see quite clearly that Rob loves the story and the characters and escapes into the world. He is comfortable with words like "Chuunin," yet does not know what "scornful" means. Rob is a familiar picture to many teachers; if we take the time to find out what our students love, as many teachers already do, we could bridge a literacy achievement gap.

ASSESSING NEW SKILLS FROM NEW TEXTS

There are particular ways of assessing skills that emerge from the new texts that students use and enjoy. Eve Bearne and her team in England have devised an assessment framework to assess new literacies skills. Bearne claims that we need to have dialogues that will help children recognize the different representational demands made by different texts. Using Bearne's assessment framework is a way forward in assessing students like Rob.

Composition and Effect: This looks at children's ability to write imaginative, interesting, and thoughtful texts and to produce texts that are appropriate to the task, reader, and purposes:

- Select and adapt form and content according to purpose, viewpoint, and reader
- Convey ideas and themes in appropriate styles.

Text Structure and Organization: This focuses on children's ability to organize and present whole texts effectively, sequencing and structuring information, ideas, and events, constructing paragraphs, and using cohesion within and between paragraphs:

- Select and use structural devices for the organization of texts
- Order and group ideas and material within sections of their texts to elaborate meaning
- Maintain cohesion in texts of increasing variety and complexity

Sentence Structure and Punctuation: This considers children's ability to write with technical accuracy of syntax and punctuation in phrases, clauses, and sentences for clarity, purpose, and effect:

- Select and deploy a variety and complex range of sentence structures
- Use punctuation to mark grammatical boundaries and clarify meaning accurately and consistently
- Combine grammatical structure and punctuation to enhance meaning
- Use correct spelling

(Bearne et al, 2004; 2005).

Bearne and her colleagues use this framework to evaluate and assess a series of different multimodal texts. The term *multimodal* refers to an approach to literacy that argues that students use different kinds of modes that are equally visual, written, interactive, aural, and kinetic, and that they're understanding of different modes informs the way that they learn. Most texts nowadays are more than written words and, as such, require different kinds of skills (and different ways of assessing these skills).

A History of New Literacies

The concept of new kinds of literacy that our students bring to classrooms takes its roots from New Literacy Studies, a field of research and practice that brings together the disciplines of anthropology, sociology, semiotics, and linguistics to study literacy in different places by different kinds of people. New Literacy Studies (NLS) grew out of an increasing need to account for a literacy achievement gap that could not be explained within literacy education alone, as literacy scholars expanded their perspective on literacy by consulting scholars in other disciplines.

"There are global matters of swift communications through Internet, e-mail, and digital imaging ... and surrounding us are daily reminders that news media, advertising—all the rhetorical devices of society—are using image plus language in increasingly complex ways ... These changes impose urgent demands on educational practice in literacy."
— Eva Bearne

Several NLS studies, such as those conducted by Shirley Brice Heath, Brian Street, and David Barton and Mary Hamilton, illustrated that literacy takes place everywhere, all of the time—only not exactly in ways that we think of when we think of school literacy (Heath, 1983; Street, 1993; Barton & Hamilton, 1998). What each study showed was that children, frequently from different cultures and challenging economic situations, had a variety of ways of using language in meaningful ways. In Heath's study, an African-American community drew on oral language and oral retellings of stories to make meaning (Heath, 1983). Street's study showed that there were three different models of literacy in a community in Iran: one tied to mosque and Islamic teachings; one tied to British schooling; and one tied to secular ways of speaking and understanding. Only one of these literacies is tied to schooling, yet they all represent ways of making meaning with language. Finally, Barton and Hamilton offered a longitudinal study of the literacy habits of hundreds of people in Lancaster to powerfully show the variety of ways in which we read, write, think, create, listen, and speak. Each scholar blazed a trail for us to rethink what literacy is and how it is shaped by people, places, and practices.

New Literacy Studies opened up literacy and, as educators, we can build on the strength of it:

- by using our students' literacy in the home to foster their reading and writing development;
- by seeing that every child comes with a "fund of knowledge" (see page 51) that we need to figure out and harness to our teaching;
- by appreciating that literacy is far more complex than accepted models of good literacy teaching practice, such as paired reading or guided reading (although both of these strategies are important as well).

The "new" in new literacy is an approach to literacy teaching and learning that acknowledges how we all come at literacy from different perspectives and how, as literacy leaders and educators, we need to find ways of mediating the different experiences and identities of our students.

Some valuable studies have grown out of the New Literacy Studies tradition, such as the work of Don Leu and his colleagues. In their work, they shift the concept of "new" to skills that students develop from their use of technology. New literacies can therefore imply the novel nature of many of the digital practices we have acquired, such as using search engines like Google or constructing and maintaining a page in MySpace. Our students spend a lot of time in digital spaces, and scholars such as Leu (Leu & Coiro, 2004) and Knobel and Lankshear (Knobel & Lankshear, 2007) examine in some detail how these practices inform our understanding of contemporary literacy.

> **Using New Literacies in the Classroom**
>
> 1. Literacy happens everywhere all of the time. As educators, we need to find out what our students do at home and outside of school.
> 2. Children have expertise about things that they value. Incorporate different kinds of texts and artifacts into teaching and display them in your teaching space.
> 3. Literacy can be broken down into four essential components: the meaning-maker, the text, the context, and the practice.
> 4. Our own cultures and backgrounds inform our teaching — and, of course, student learning.
> 5. Culture and cultural practice is a lens through which we see, hear, and visualize things.

Critical Literacy

In conjunction with a redefining of literacy came efforts to look more critically at our perceptions of literacy. The work of Paolo Freire was instrumental in looking at issues of power within literacy and what literacy can do for people (Freire & Macedo, 1987). Freire is famous for claiming that reading the word is key to reading the world. After Freire, we saw the ascendance of critical literacy as a key topic in literacy education; that is, taking a critical look at ways we use literacy and how literacy gives people currency. Many literacy scholars have taken up a critical approach to how our students learn literacy, so that students can unpeel the layers and complexity of language, spoken or written.

Critical literacy as a field argues that students at all levels of education need to have a meta-awareness of how language functions in different genres of texts and in different contexts. Critical literacy compels teachers of literacy to explore the structures of stories and nuances of characterizations, but also the register of language, the choice of words, and the origins of texts and practices used around texts. The critical aspect of critical literacy deals with how we frame our reading of texts so that we see where our interpretation begins and ends, and where meanings within texts begin and end (akin to Rosenblatt's Reader Response Theory, 2005). An approach to critical literacy curriculum can involve using issues of power and ideas as a lens for looking at texts. Critical literacy can also involve reading multiple texts to compare competing accounts of and stances on events, cultures, and places. Critical literacy entails working intertextually, not just across different media and genres, but also across cultural and historical texts and contexts (Luke, 2004). James Paul Gee argues that critical literacy is "socially perceptive literacy" (Gee, 1993). Luke and Freebody argue that there are certain key elements to critical literacy that encourage readers to be code breakers, meaning makers, text users, and text critics. Barbara Comber maintains that critical literacy means practicing the use of language in powerful ways to get things done in the world (Comber, 2007).

Cultural Literacies

Our students bring a host of experiences when they come to our classrooms. Every one of them comes with culture — race, religion, family experiences, routines, treasured texts and artifacts — and it is up to us as educators to figure out exactly what these features of their lives are so that we understand how they make meaning. Gunther Kress argues that we cannot understand students' way into print unless we understand the processes of their meaning-making (Kress, 1997). Cultural literacies are plural because so many of our students (and we) carry multiple cultures with them. Appreciating the pluralistic composition of our classrooms fosters ease and a sense of belonging. Gonzales, Moll, and Amanti talk about *funds of knowledge* that we bring with us from our cultures and our homes. These funds we carry with us and they inform the way in which we learn. Funds of knowledge are the cultural artifacts and bodies of knowledge that underlie household activities (Gonzales, Moll, & Amanti, 2005). They are inherent cultural resources found in communities surrounding schools.

> Understanding and acknowledging our students' cultural literacies — as in different languages, religion, and habits of mind that they carry with them — is a key way of understanding their meaning-making.

WHAT ARE CULTURAL RESOURCES?

Cultural resources signify the cultural worlds of our students. They are important and need to be present in some guise in our classroom spaces and to be used, to varying degrees, in our planning. The term "culture" is used in the broadest sense in this instance. Cultural resources invite us into student worlds.

- Objects in the home: e.g., cushions, blankets, chairs from which children make meaning.
- Arts and crafts: paper, different kinds of paint, markers, scissors, glue, clay, brushes, crayons, etc.
- Family artifacts: mementos, symbols, old jewelry, clothes tied to events (e.g., saris), heirlooms, dress-up clothes, family tokens that have become a part of family history and signify ways of being in the family.
- Religious texts: religious texts and artifacts that tell stories and are written in a certain way that students understand.
- Popular culture: bedspreads, posters, CD covers, etc. that speak to student interests.
- New media: handheld computers, smaller console games, and game cards.

Cultural literacies exist within school communities as well. There are often dominant cultures within school communities, and it is important to use the halls and walls of your school to acknowledge cultures. Translating newsletters and school correspondence is one way of speaking to cultures within your school's community.

- Toys: Lego, puzzles, maps, action figures, Barbies, etc.
- Stuff: baskets, masks, binoculars, little soldiers, etc.

LINKING CULTURAL RESOURCES WITH LITERACY

- Plot meaning-making: In an early-years classroom, have student chart objects that they have made to reveal how different children are making meaning in the classroom.
- Play and writing: Let children value their writing and see its relationship to play.
- Understand internal signs: Children each have a unique pathway into literacy. To foster this pathway, have students use whatever mode they like (visual, written, three-dimensional, dramatic play) to complete a task, such as creating a summary of the story just read.
- Gallery walk: Set up the classroom like a gallery; have students walk around to look at each other's works of art and talk about how they made them.
- Listening to children: Listening to children's talk while they are making meaning can tell you a great deal about what interests them, how they learn, and what modes they prefer or privilege over others.
- Making links: It is essential to make links between artifacts that children create in the classroom and how they are progressing with their reading and writing broadly, and how the same skills they have used in production cross over into their reading and writing specifically.
- Works-in-progress: As formative assessment, keep track of what students are working on and how these works change as they get closer to completion.
- Bringing home into school: As Kate Pahl expresses it, "Be aware that models made at home may have deep significance for the child." Have students talk about their model-making at home and help them see the tie between work they do at school and the kinds of activities that they do at home.
- Diversify texts: After reading a story, have students use cultural resources to extend story ideas. For example, in a story about a girl who lives in a hotel and who is very naughty and rides the elevator, have students create a diorama of a scene from the movie *Eloise*.
- Parents as a cultural resource: Have a parent come to class to discuss why a particular artifact is important to their family.

As Barbara Comber sagely advises, "the local and specific nature of children's lives will always influence what teachers of critical literacy believe is needed and is possible" (Comber & Nixon, 2005: 130). What is needed and certainly possible is an acknowledgement of the stuff that presides over our students' meaning-making. Using family literacy practices or popular culture as resources will open up our teaching to our students' worlds.

Multiliteracies and Digital Literacies

With the rethinking of literacy and the acknowledgment of multiple kinds of literacy, there has been an opening up about what we mean by literacy. The term "multimodality" has gained some ground as a more contemporary way of describing the ways in which our students make meaning out in the world. Multimodality represents the different elements of texts of all kinds from which we make meaning. Texts are no longer solely made up of words and occasionally pictures, but instead are often a patchwork of other kinds of modalities that we understand alone or in combination.

Multimodal theory has influenced two new and important fields of research: multiliteracies and digital literacies. As literacy principals, you need to be acquainted with them to meet your students halfway.

Multiliteracies was launched at a meeting with key literacy scholars. From the meeting emerged a framework and new way of thinking about literacy. Multiliteracies scholars (Cope & Kalantzis, 2000) contend that literacy is far more about design than it is about written words. They argue that literacy, broken down, requires using available designs to design texts — and requires redesigning them how we see fit. Their framework argues that we need to situate our teaching within students' worlds, that we should teach overtly to the skills that they bring to school and, of course, critically frame these skills. Multiliteracies is a way for us to think about the new ways we read and make texts in light of technology and the prominent role of digital spaces in our students' lives.

Digital literacies represent another field of research that looks in detail at digital spaces and how we make meaning within them. Scholars working in digital literacies (Davies & Merchant, 2007; Carrington, 2006) look at digital texts — such as blogs, wikis, or zines — and break apart what these texts do, how they are made, and the kinds of skills that they imply.

Thinking About New Literacies: A Checklist

- ❏ I am speaking to skills students possess (e.g., cultural literacies; funds of knowledge; modalities in their work and in texts that they enjoy).
- ❏ I have accounted for issues of gender in my teaching, in my choice of texts, and the ways in which we use these texts.
- ❏ I have thought about funds of knowledge that my students bring to the classroom.
- ❏ I have accounted for multimodality in the texts that I use.
- ❏ I have thought about the benefits certain texts afford over others (e.g., a pop-up book gives students a sense of three-dimensionality and offers more materiality than other kinds of books).
- ❏ I am situating my teaching in student worlds and critically framing the material that I teach.
- ❏ I am aware of my own identity and cultural literacies and how they inform my teaching.
- ❏ I acknowledge that students come in with a host of experiences and it is my job to find them out.

Cueing Systems for Reading

Reading is an interactive process in which the reader uses a variety of strategies for ensuring that comprehension occurs. In order to make meaning in print, all readers blend four cueing systems: pragmatic, semantic, syntactic, and phonographemic (phonics). Pragmatic and semantic cues help readers to use syntax and language patterns to predict words and phrases; phonics cues help readers to test predictions for unrecognized or confusing words in order to construct or confirm meaning.

It is important to help young readers become aware of how using the various cueing systems can help them find meaning in text and support their reading growth. Young children already have some of these strategies, and may use them to figure out individual words or phrases. The process is more complicated, however, when they must apply strategies to words embedded in a text, especially unfamiliar words within text that is outside their frame of experience.

A reader uses the four cueing systems simultaneously to varying degrees. Proficient readers use a minimum of cues, while less experienced readers or readers who are reading a text for a specific purpose may use more cues to help them determine meaning. Limited readers often tend to use phonics cues as their primary strategy. When these readers are reading difficult texts, they, in essence, may need to decode the majority of words they meet. This limits the amount of comprehension that occurs as a result of the reading — the more a child must decode individual words in a text, the less meaning she or he may take away from the experience.

A proficient reader's recognition of words is so immediate and vast that they rarely notice their use of context cues. Their rate of recognition is directly tied to the amount of reading they do — the more a reader reads, the greater the automatic sight vocabulary. A parallel situation exists for those who read a variety of types of text — as they increase their exposure to text types, their recognition of patterns and structures specific to a genre of text increases. Knowledge of patterns is reinforced when writing is combined with reading — children then have the opportunity to put into practice their awareness of how print works. However, even proficient readers may sometimes miss interesting turns of phrases or special nuances because they are processing text at a speed that does not allow for subtleties. Revisiting or working with the text may increase both comprehension and the metacognitive awareness of experience of the text.

It has been proven that strong literacy programs at the primary levels that incorporate all four cueing systems can dramatically reduce the number of reading problems experienced by today's adolescents and young adults. To do this, educators need to focus on the following core elements of literacy teaching:

- Alphabet knowledge
- Knowledge of sound–letter correspondences
- Automatic sight words
- Reading for meaning
- Numerous opportunities for reading many types of books and digital resources
- Increased teaching time and extra resources devoted to at-risk readers
- A secure environment that encourages children to grow as readers and writers using a variety of texts and text forms

Critical Comprehension

When readers read, are they always able to make sense of what they are seeing in print, both on the page and onscreen? Do they connect to what the author is saying or do they think about what she or he is saying? Are the author's words or ideas too far removed from their own experiences? The question remains for teachers: How can they assist children in making sense of what they read, so that their personal understanding and satisfaction will grow and deepen from the experience? This is what is meant by "teaching comprehension."

Reading comprehension or textual understanding occurs when readers are able to interpret written symbols in order to make meaning. A reader internalizes the accrued meanings and relates these to previous knowledge, experiences, and texts read before. Comprehension is a cognitive, emotional process, and thus, it is difficult to assess. Yet its presence or absence can be determined to some extent when teachers

- Watch and listen to students reading a text
- Ask students to describe what they have read
- Discuss books that students are reading with them
- Encourage students to share their responses to what they have read

Everyone's experience differs. It is important for teachers to keep this reality in mind as they work with groups so that they don't present only one interpretation of a story. Instead, teachers must share their expertise in such ways that support students and encourage their learning.

In order for readers to understand a text, they must be able to relate it to other texts they have read and to life experiences, thereby combining the knowledge gained from this text to their knowledge base. The strength of these connections relates directly to students' level of comprehension. If students cannot connect the reading to personal aspects of their lives, their level of comprehension will suffer, just as it will if they cannot connect the text to others they have read.

As will be discussed in more depth in Chapter 4, these informal ways to assess students' comprehension can be combined with more formal assessments to provide teachers with a picture of students' levels of comprehension with particular texts. Teachers can then assist children with strategies that enhance comprehension, helping them make meaning before they read, as they read, and after they read.

Stages of Reading

Most students follow what can be considered a continuum of reading acquisition; however, they do not always master skills in order. That is, they may have difficulty with one strategy, yet will have gained another typically evidenced by a more fluent reader. Competencies vary according to the text being read and the situations in which they find themselves reading.

When teachers assess students' reading ability, they need to consider where the majority of the behaviors fall on a particular place in the continuum. Then, they need to watch that students make gains that will move them into the next stage of reading.

Students progress at their own rate and in their own style. In the past, readers who progressed at a slower rate were often labeled (e.g., learning disabled, dyslexic, attention deficit disorder). However, it is now known that if teachers can identify the various stages of growth, then they can have a much clearer picture of the problems and what each needs to do to build strength as a reader.

Since reading is an individual process, one of the best indicators a teacher can use to assess a child's growth is his or her own development throughout the year. In order to do this, it is necessary to establish a baseline of skills and knowledge.

In this way, as teachers assess students through the year, they can return to the baseline to see where each student has made gains.

The sections that follow provide a brief overview of the five stages of reading to help establish the baseline of skills and knowledge referred to above.

The Early Reader

Early readers, who are sometimes referred to as pre-readers, enter Kindergarten with some of the skills and concepts they need to become readers. These children generally enjoy reading, since most of their experiences with texts have involved being read to by family members or caregivers. Books, then, represent pleasure and entertainment for them. Many children will have favorite stories they like to hear again and again. These readers have a sense of story and enter into stories readily.

Early readers will often pick up a book and approximate reading by holding it the right way, stopping the reading while they turn the page, and finishing the story exactly on the last page. Such imitation is not without value. Through this, children learn that texts give readers cues to reading, that print on a page matches certain words, that pictures support the story, that books are read from front to back, that text flows from left to right, and that reading is an authentic activity. When children "read" books in this way, they are preparing themselves to become readers.

Early readers know that print carries meaning and they are aware of sources of print around them — in books, on products, on labels, on signs, etc. While they recognize many of these words in context, they may not carry over this knowledge when they see the words in isolation. These readers may not know how sounds are represented by letters. Phonemic awareness (how sounds combine to make words) and phonics (how words are written on a page) will develop during this period.

Phonemic and phonics instruction, if it is to be effective, should occur through real reading activities, such as using rhymes, songs, patterns, and word games. These activities focus children's attention on sounds and the corresponding letter or letters that represent them. It is only when children have a knowledge of sound–letter correspondence that they can begin to read and write independently and transfer knowledge from one situation to another.

The Emergent Reader

Emergent readers, like early readers, enjoy listening to stories and have favorite books that they seemingly never tire of. Children at this stage know that books can provide them with entertainment and information, and they see themselves as capable of reading them.

These youngsters have refined their knowledge of how books work, and realize that the purpose of print is to record or share meaning, and that it is fixed. They are beginning to rely on semantic and syntactic cueing systems to predict events, and can retell sequences of events. These children are interested in developing their print abilities. They like to have their stories transcribed, which they can read back to a teacher or parent.

To help emergent readers develop knowledge of how writing reflects spoken words, it is necessary to create environments where children are surrounded by print. Teachers or parents need to show examples of how print is used and give children plenty of opportunities to read books successfully, particularly pattern books and books with detailed illustrations. Shared reading, of course, brings these books alive and directs children to focus on functions of print. Finally, publishing children's own stories gives them real reasons to write and reinforces the major purposes of writing — to record and to share.

The Transitional Reader

Developing or transitional readers can read some texts independently and successfully. Children at this stage of reading often enjoy books by a favorite author, including books in a series, and it is during this period that children come to recognize characteristics of various genres. Using this knowledge, and their experience in reading, they begin to develop a personal literary taste.

At this stage, their knowledge of sound–letter correspondence is growing, and they can recognize and write letter groups such as blends and digraphs. Their knowledge of sight words is also growing, and they can read these words in both familiar and unfamiliar contexts.

As they read, developing readers use all four cueing systems to help them make meaning. They are able to self-monitor their reading, identifying and correcting miscues, and can substitute words that make sense when they are unsure of a text. At this level children are reading silently. Some children may still finger-point or say the words softly to themselves. As their reading ability develops further, they will discontinue these practices.

To progress in their literacy development, developing readers need to consolidate a strong sense of story. Teachers can build upon developing readers' enjoyment of independent reading, particularly with familiar texts, as well as their interest in discussing stories in small groups, and the value they place on connections between reading and writing. As part of their literacy program, teachers should introduce chapter books and simple novels, and ask students to retell the plots of stories they have read. To imbue a meta-awareness of texts, children at this stage need to be encouraged to recognize characteristics of genres of texts. As well, they need to increase knowledge of literary elements and the materiality of texts (e.g., the cover, illustrations, etc.). Developing readers should also recognize phonics generalizations and have a growing vocabulary.

Texts for Learning Readers

Lea Pelletier

The content area teachers with whom I work have struggled for years with students who won't read their textbooks as assigned. When I went into some of the textbooks looking for strategies that might help, I found that the majority of them had readability levels that suited only fluent readers, and that did not use text features at all well (either too few, or so many that they distracted from the "meat," graphics that didn't really help at all).

When I sat down and talked with the teachers about this, most were incredibly relieved; they had thought they were incompetent because they couldn't motivate the students to do the reading. Since then, we have used a number of strategies to help students through parts of the existing textbooks; however, we have also spent considerable time successfully locating alternative or supplementary texts for the units they teach. At first, some of them experienced concern that this was "dumbing down"; but about three weeks ago, one of them who teaches a course often taken by marginal readers stopped me in the hall and said, "I'm completely converted. I just finished the unit on _____ with the book we bought last spring, and I was able to cover three times the content, and they know it!"

I've done PD sessions on this issue across the region and at a provincial conference; in it, I place teachers in the students' position, and give them a short text to read on astrophysics, with a short test to complete in table teams. They struggle for a while and exhibit all the behavior that you see in a classroom when students can't read. Then I give them a "friendlier" text that contains all the same content, but is more simply written and is laid out better; with this text, of course, they succeed. They guess that the first text had a readability level between Grades 14 and 16, and that the second was about Grade 10; I tell them that the first was at Grade 11.9, and the second, Grade 6.3. Then we talk about what this means for their teaching. It has been powerful.

I really believe that, while we want all students to be fluent readers and continue to work hard toward that goal, in secondary school we cannot, in all conscience, keep bright students who have problems with reading from acquiring the content they are capable of understanding by giving them textbooks from which they cannot make meaning.

The Fluent Reader

Fluent readers have arrived at a point where they have built up an extensive sight vocabulary and thus are free from the time-consuming word analysis that may have occurred at previous stages. These readers can read a range of texts for a variety of purposes, read silently, link new information with existing knowledge, and adjust their style of reading to reflect the type of book being read.

This is a critical stage in reading. Some children may begin to lose their enthusiasm for reading because books may appear too challenging or they no longer find themselves as captivated by story. In these cases, we must select books that children enjoy and that they can read successfully, all the while avoiding habits and classroom routines that may give reading activities the "appearance" of a choice (e.g., routine comprehension questions). Children need to continue to confirm reading as an act that entertains them, that brings them satisfaction, that adds to their knowledge, and that is undertaken for genuine reasons.

Just as they are becoming independent in their reading, so, too, are they becoming independent in their writing. These children are learning to write in a variety of forms for a variety of audiences and purposes. In addition, they are improving the quality of their written work through editing and proofreading, and are mastering the conventions of the language.

The school's role is to help children develop those strategies that will increase their reading and writing fluency. Teachers can do this in part by identifying genres that appear appealing, by demonstrating behaviors they consider useful (e.g., proofreading written material), by conferring with children on an as-needed basis, and by acting as a resource to help them rediscover the joys of reading.

The Independent Reader

Independent readers read texts independently and silently. The style of reading they choose reflects the material being read and these readers monitor their reading for understanding.

These children can read a range of books, as well as novels that reflect other cultures, other times, and other ways of looking at the world. They are capable of interpreting complex plots and characterization, and need to be challenged to move ahead on their own, using fiction, non-fiction, and computers.

To further the development of independent readers, it is important to encourage them to read a range of texts in a variety of ways, through such means as independent reading, shared reading, and literature circles. Since their writing often reflects their reading knowledge, they can be encouraged to respond to texts read in innovative ways.

English Language Learners

"The current literacy initiatives and practices in Aboriginal education are varied to suit the needs of many students, teachers, and schools, and are all developed with the intention of providing an educationally rich environment where all students will learn to read and write. In order to achieve this, we must foster a shared decision-making process that invites and supports a partnership with the Aboriginal community so that students will feel respected and connected to the learning environment." — Vancouver School Board

These ELL readers face a special challenge. Although they share their peers' reading tastes, their level of English precludes them from reading many age-appropriate texts. These children generally do not want to read books that are read by younger children. High-interest low-vocabulary novels were developed to fill this gap, but did not prove to be a great success, with their general lack of plot and character sophistication. What then do teachers give these children that will appeal to their humor, their sense of adventure, and their thirst for a good story? How do schools teach them to read?

First, teachers need to realize that it is important to honor each child's culture. By providing an atmosphere where these students see their past experiences as valuable to their learning of English, they have in place a set of skills and a knowledge bank on which they can draw as they learn the language. Indeed they may benefit from being able to speak and write in their home language as they become accustomed to their new surroundings.

Second, it is essential to welcome these children into the school and make them feel a part of the school culture. Where possible, teachers may wish to pair a child with no English with a child who shares the same home language but who has acquired some English. This buddy can introduce the new child to the physical layout of the school, its schedule, its resources, and its extracurricular activities, as well as provide a model for language-acquisition success.

Finally, it is imperative that ELL readers get experience with more than just simple texts. By giving these children the same books that others are reading,

Each year, principal Ann Christy had beautiful and intricate designs painted on her arms by parents in her school's ethnic community. She also invited guests from the community, such as singers, storytellers, and authors, to come to the school. These were important components of the celebrations in her multicultural urban school.

then structuring the learning so that they can receive assistance and support as they read, you can ensure these students can sustain interest while advancing their language skills.

The Reader in Difficulty

The factors that explain why some students are at-risk readers are as varied as the children themselves. Some may have medical difficulties, challenges at home, or attention deficit difficulties that impede their learning, while others may learn at a slower rate than their peers, including both those experiencing problems in particular areas or in all areas of learning. Some students may progress at a "normal" pace for a while, but become blocked at a particular point in their learning. Whatever the reason, teachers need to observe and assess these students to decide on the support they most need.

Teachers can often help these students by spending time with them individually or, for brief times, in small groups where they share the same level of literacy development as others. It is of particular importance to read aloud to these students, to read with them, and to listen to them read. Teachers can also assist at-risk readers by giving them quiet reading time, by helping them to identify the purposes for reading, and by making obvious the link to activities that make experiences with print meaningful and real.

Boys and Literacy

This issue is discussed at length in *Even Hockey Players Read* by David Booth.

When we began researching material about boys and literacy, we were amazed at the quantity of available resources for parents and teachers, especially on the Internet. People are certainly concerned about males and literacy. Dozens of books have emerged in the last few years documenting issues in male culture and in raising and schooling boys. Some emphasize biological differences in males and females; others take a socio-constructivist approach; still others struggle for a culturally elitist model promoting the literary canon. We need to look at them all to find directions for supporting parents, teachers, and educational policy makers, but especially for helping youngsters themselves to begin taking control of their literacy lives, aware of their own needs and interests as developing readers and writers.

Consider the change in the texts we read today at home or work: books of every variety — softcover and hardback; thousands and thousands of magazines and comics available from the local newsstand; letters, bills, ads, and pamphlets through the mailbox; electronic print of all sorts, from ones that fit in the palm to giant TV screens; memos, fact sheets, documents, e-mail and attachments. The definition of literacy has altered, as have the strategies necessary for reading text.

Before deciding on plans of action, we need to examine the issues pertaining to the literacy lives of boys, how they perceive themselves as readers, and how parents, teachers, and peers influence their literacy development. The role of gender in reading success is complex, and we want to uncover many of the assumptions and stereotypes that parents and educators have about boys and how they handle the world of print text. We need to listen to the voices of writers for young people, of authorities in this field, and, most crucially, of boys and men as they reveal their literacy challenges, struggles, tastes, and values, and offer us insights into how we can support all learners in their literacy journeys.

If we believe that all children should have access to the literacy world, how will we ensure that boys, in particular, see themselves as readers who can handle the requirements of such a variety of texts? Non-readers tell us too many stories of punishment and pain, of no care and no touch, where books never metamorphosed into friendly objects, where worksheets and controlled readers dictated their eye movements and caused their reading hearts to beat irregularly. They drown in printer's ink.

We don't want to generate or fuel new problems for education — especially for girls — as we explore and even promote programs for boys. And there are diverse opinions about the origin and even the nature of the problems that we find inside such a discussion. Most importantly, the education of boys is closely connected to the education of girls, and school and education policies on gender will directly influence both. If we focus on the problems of boys, do we endanger the efforts of so many in the struggle to bring equity for girls into our society? Or do we see these initiatives as dialogues that are attempting to move us all forward into strengthening the lives of every child as an individual? What if we refuse to consider the issues not as a "war," but as an inquiry into the dynamics of how boys and girls construct their gendered literacy lives?

How can we who work in schools respond fairly to the needs of boys in relation to the needs of girls, and to the diversity among groups of boys and girls? Fortunately, we can benefit from the educational reforms that grew from the changes associated with girls: we can apply those principles of gender equity to the educational needs of boys, even though in many ways that very system of schooling formerly marginalized girls and privileged some boys. What conditions, then, contain or exacerbate these problems for so many boys and for many girls?

We know that no single category includes all boys or all girls. We don't need to add to the stereotype of classifying all boys' behaviors, tastes, and attitudes into one single frame, nor do we want to reinforce the generalities that are often applied to boys. But as we look at studies and reports that examine boys and girls, their learning styles and special interests, their growth patterns and their stages of intellectual development, we do notice differences. These differences are not in all boys or in all girls, but in enough of them to cause us to reflect about our demands on their young lives.

At a school we recently visited, we observed that twice a week at noon hour, the principal plays basketball with those Grade 7 and 8 boys who are working in a group for troubled readers. The activity is a strong motivating force for the students.

There are definite problems with the ways in which many boys view themselves as literate beings, with how they approach the acts of reading and writing, and with how they respond to assessments of their skills. At least the faltering test scores have opened up discussion on these issues that concern many teachers and parents.

How closely are we watching and interpreting the alarmist data? Are all boys at risk? If not, which ones? How significant are developmental stages in boys' literacy abilities? Are there differences in boys' growth with boys of the same age? What is normal literacy achievement for a six-year-old boy? Is it the same for a six-year-old girl? Which boy and which girl? Are we concerned about the girls who are doing poorly? And most important, what do we mean by "literacy"?

Parents and teachers have many questions, and they are almost always about boys in literacy trouble: they don't read, can't read, won't read, don't write, can't write, can't spell. Those of us who are responsible for educating boys are deeply concerned over the plight of many of them who can't or won't enter the literacy club. But our rules for entry are very strict and, oddly enough, computer skills are seldom part of the qualifications.

We need to examine the challenging issues around boys and literacy. The role of gender in learning to read and write is complex, and educators need to uncover many of the stereotypes we hold as parents and teachers about boys and how they cope with the world of print, so that we can create and support a culture of literacy in school and at home that engages boys who can't read, who don't read, and who *do* read.

Strategies for Boys' Literacy Success
Ontario Ministry of Education

1. Be in their corner: The role of the teacher in supporting boys' literacy
2. Keep it real: Making reading and writing authentic and relevant to boys
3. Have the right stuff: Choosing appropriate classroom resources for boys
4. Help make it a habit: Providing frequent opportunities to read and write
5. Let them talk: Appealing to boys' need for social interaction
6. Teach with purpose: Understanding boys' learning styles
7. Read between the lines: Bringing critical literacy skills into the classroom
8. Get the Net: Using technology to get boys interested in literacy
9. Embrace the arts: Using the arts to bring literacy to life
10. Find positive role models: Influencing boys' attitudes through the use of role models
11. Drive the point home: Engaging parents in boys' literacy
12. Build a school-wide focus: Extending literacy beyond the classroom
13. Assess for success: Using appropriate assessment tools for boys

---

Appropriate Levels of Literacy Challenge

In order to assist students in their literacy development, we need to ensure that students have access to texts that are accessible and that they can comprehend, so that they can engage in purposeful reading and responding. Students need to read for a reason — for enjoyment, for information, or for instruction, and, as they participate in making meaning with a text, they also have opportunities to learn about how they function as readers and writers, and how the process of literacy works for them.

As teachers, we want to find texts that will both engage the reader and develop literacy competence. As students apply the strategies they have acquired to new or difficult texts, they are improving and extending their reading abilities. Therefore we have to provide texts that are appropriate to the students' stage of development and to their reading interests. To achieve this, we need a variety of engaging texts that correspond with the range of student literacy competencies found in a regular classroom setting.

The texts we use in our classrooms need to represent a continuum of challenge, based on a variety of factors, so that we can match the complexity of the selection with the ability of the student. In this way, we can provide the students with guided reading lessons and conferences that support their processing of text, with only a few challenges involving word solving and issues of context and content. Students are able to see themselves as successful readers who are engaging with meaningful texts, both on the page and onscreen.

As a secondary principal, Tom Moore has a strong literacy push in his school that is built upon his own teaching career, when he filled his classroom with books. An avid reader, he purchases several hard-covered novels each month that he then donates to the school library to support young people as readers. He encourages teachers to search the newspaper for articles, editorials, and pictures that highlight their particular discipline and to mount them on bulletin boards each day. This way, students can note the contemporary effect of literacy in their lives.

In a school with a mandate for improving literacy for all students, the library should become the main focus in building a central resource to support every student and every teacher. Today's school libraries can supply invaluable texts for enriching the literacy lives of the students: computer resources, information books, novels for both boys and girls, magazines, poetry anthologies, and reference materials. Through the collections and resources an effective library offers, each classroom becomes connected to the world outside the school, and the teacher/librarian can add support to every teacher's programs — in curriculum areas, during independent reading, for student research projects, and, most of all, by motivating and encouraging students to widen their literacy horizons and to deepen their awareness of the great variety of texts, both in print and online, that will connect them to that world.

The New Literacies, as they have been labeled, are concerned with multimodal texts such as comics, magazines, newspapers, books, the Internet, e-mail, graphics, video, and sound. Together, these texts fill the lives of our students, and meaning is accrued as students combine the messages from the different media into their own construct of the world.

Selecting Quality Literacy Resources

Questions for Selecting Resources

- Reviewing new materials to meet needs
- How are school teams involved in selection
- How are student data used in selection
- What process is in place for gap analysis

Outcomes

- Incorporates a variety of organizational structures
- Whole-class, small-group, and independent instruction
- Offers multiple perspectives
- Linguistic, social, and cultural diversity
- Connects to student lives, knowledge, and experiences
- Relevant to student interests
- Encourages curiosity
- Matched to assessed needs and strengths
- Promotes technology and media
- Promotes critical literacy
- Encourages higher-order thinking
- Increasingly complex topics and issues
- Aligned with curricula
- Cross-curricular connections
- Explore a variety of text forms
- Aligned with new initiatives for improving achievement
- Includes assessment for learning, strategies, and tools
- Consistent with current research about literacy practice
- Interconnects the language arts
- Provides purposeful, direct instruction, demonstrations, and modeling
- Supports the gradual release of responsibility to the students

---

The Graphic Novel

Many of today's young readers enjoy reading a type of book different from those that we are most familiar with — the graphic novel. This shouldn't come as a surprise in a world where visuals from TV, videos, games, and computers fill so much of our youngsters' time. In an increasingly image-filled culture, this new literacy medium offers alternatives to traditional texts used in schools, while at the same time promoting literacy development. For many of us, comics are tainted as a lesser genre, relegated to childhood's Saturday-morning leisure time. But many of today's graphic novels include a complex and art-filled variety of genres, from fiction to biography, social studies and science, representing social, economic, and political themes and topics that readers might not choose in other types of texts. As well, they present opportunities for incorporating media literacy into the reading program, as students critically examine this word-and-image medium itself.

The concept of the graphic novel is conveyed through two separate terms: "novel" and "graphic." The concept of *novel* is generally understood as a form of literature, popular among readers, and well-used by authors of textual narratives in English and other languages throughout the world. The *Oxford English Dictionary* defines a novel as "a fictitious prose narrative or tale of considerable length... in which characters and actions representative of the real life of past or present time are portrayed in a plot of more or less complexity." *Graphic novel* is a branch of this literary form. In simple words, a graphic novel may be described as a stand-alone and complete narrative (story) presented through texts and pictures in parallel with the definition of the term *graphic*, "the production of pictures, diagrams, etc., in association with text."

The Intervention Process

Research shows that there are certain factors that affect literacy. These include

- Poor readers read less than their peers
- Poor readers are constrained by a lack of vocabulary development and world knowledge
- Poor readers often experience reading in negative, passive, and inefficient ways

Based on studies of large-scale initiatives over the past decade, such as Slavin's Success for All, Reading Recovery™, and Crevola and Hill's Early Years Literacy Project, the earlier you intervene with at-risk readers, the greater the improvement. Early intervention has repeatedly been shown to have a substantial impact on children's reading progress.

According to Jane Hurry of the Institute of Education in Great Britain, research evidence demonstrates that successful reading interventions require

- One-to-one tutoring in a broad curriculum
- The inclusion of different genres of texts in a variety of groupings
- The incorporation of writing, particularly related to spelling and word-level work
- Explicit phonics teaching connected to the content of the text

In her article, Hurry maintains that, although we need to acknowledge the contributions of meaning-based reading by always having a language context, there has to be a phonological element to any intervention.

In identifying a framework for intervention, it is important to focus on the following aspects:

- An intensive literacy program
- Effective teaching
- Assessment

An Intensive Literacy Program

An intensive literacy program includes a combination of phonics teaching alongside meaningful and purposeful literacy activities. There are certain key principles that are fundamental to this approach:

- Understanding that print carries a message
- Learning the relationship between letters and sounds
- Developing sight vocabulary
- Learning letter formations and spellings for writing

- Monitoring comprehension and inference skills

Some of the more successful interventions have been ones that merge a phonological approach with a meaning-based approach. What is also increasingly important is a writing component, including spelling awareness.

Effective Teaching

Research and practice have shown us that one-to-one teaching instruction in reading and writing is the best vehicle for success in literacy. As discussed above, intervention programs should also be intensive and instituted as early as possible.

The following are the critical issues in terms of teaching strategies for reading interventions:

- Increase the amount of time devoted to teaching literacy
- Use a one-to-one approach, as it has been proven more reliable than group programs
- Make professional development a component of the intervention process to ensure that the implementation of programs like Reading Recovery™ are an integral part of the overall school program

Assessment

Assessment should be used to inform the teaching decisions about particular interventions. Chapter 4 provides a comprehensive look at the role of assessment and evaluation in all aspects of literacy teaching.

Through assessment we not only establish what pupils know, but also what programs will fit their needs (e.g., phonemic awareness, word recognition, comprehension skills, etc.). Most importantly, assessment charts student progress. Susan Schwartz maintains that knowledge about assessment and evaluation is key to planning and monitoring all literacy initiatives.

Writing

Over a series of Saturdays during the year, principal Roy Howard drove groups of Grade 6 students to the museum in a large nearby city, followed by lunch in an interesting restaurant. The students' experiences resulted in all kinds of writing, talk, and further research, which they then shared with Roy.

Quality writing occurs in classrooms where students write about things that matter to them, and where a language-rich, supportive environment fosters their desire to see themselves as writers and increases their ability to capture their ideas and feelings proficiently. It is important for children to have real purposes for writing and to speak in their own voices with clarity and accuracy. Writing may not always be easy or fun, but it can be satisfying and purposeful.

Teachers have not always counted all of the writing events that occur in classrooms as acts of written composition, but they are. We have at least replaced the inappropriate subject term *creative writing* with *writing*, which opens the door for exploring the many different functions of writing, including reporting, creating, persuading, note-taking, and describing, to name just a few.

To encourage writing growth, teachers should encourage students to write frequently during the day in a variety of situations: for example, note-taking during a mini-lesson; working on an idea web for a social studies project; completing a final draft of an independent piece. Students need to realize that only the last type of writing mentioned here requires extensive revising and editing — that we "publish" our writing when we have something special to share and to keep. Chapter 3 describes some strategies for helping your teachers implement the writing process.

Models of Effective Literacy Programs

See The Literacy Initiative at Elms Elementary School by Theresa Licitra on page 74.

The list of programs that follows emerged from our research inquiry into literacy programs that have proven effective with students. In researching exemplary reading and writing programs, we examined three main areas:

- The philosophical framework of each program and its implications for teaching and learning
- The methodology of use required for implementation
- Assessment and evaluation components

What unites the programs we deem "effective" is a whole-school approach to changing literacy achievement in a district, state, province, or country, based on many of the components of literacy-based school change described in Chapter 1. Our selection of programs encompasses international literacy initiatives that have proven successful in Australia, Canada, Great Britain, and the United States.

See Literacy in Middle and Secondary School by Mark Federman on page 77.

We also highlight reading and writing programs that do not provide prescriptive methodologies, but instead offer guidelines for teaching practice. This approach requires professional development and support services for teachers to implement them effectively — reading and writing programs are only as effective as the principals and teachers working with them.

Each program we selected is based on an approach to the teaching of reading and writing that advocates students having ample opportunities for engaging in meaningful reading and writing activities. The programs also incorporate opportunities for students to learn through talking with others. In all of these programs, literacy skills are carefully articulated and are connected to the actual processes of reading and writing.

Administrators may wish to consult this section when considering an early reading program that fits their own and their staff's approach and/or philosophy of practice. We have divided our list of exemplary programs into three distinct models of literacy as interpretations of literacy teaching and learning:

- Balanced literacy model
- School-change model
- Literacy framework model

A Model for Balanced Literacy

A balanced literacy approach promotes reading skills and literacy among school-age children based on the characteristics of reading stages: early, emergent, developing, fluent, and independent. A balanced literacy framework entails a whole-class approach to reading development that requires strong organizational skills to assess students' learning needs, to plan instruction based on these needs, and to set up learning stations and strategies that support a literate classroom. The premise underlying programs that follow this model is that students need an environment that is organized, stimulating, and psychologically comfortable to learn effectively.

The ten components of a balanced literacy program are

1. *Read-aloud/Modeled reading* — teacher reads selection to students
2. *Shared reading* — teacher and students read text together

3. *Guided reading* — teacher introduces material at students' instructional level
4. *Interactive reading* — teacher and students read and discuss story together
5. *Independent reading* — students read independently
6. *Write-aloud/Modeled writing* — teacher models and teaches writing strategies
7. *Shared writing* — teacher and students collaborate to write and teacher acts as scribe
8. *Guided writing* — teacher reinforces writing skills and students do the writing
9. *Interactive writing* — teacher and students choose topic and compose together
10. *Independent writing* — students choose topic and write at their independent level

A balanced literacy format emphasizes speaking, listening, presenting, writing, reading, and viewing. The classroom set-up can include a whole-group area, a small-group area, and learning centres such as a reading area, a writing centre, a cross-curricular centre, computer stations, a creative arts centre, a communication area/post office, and a listening station.

A Model for School Change

Some literacy initiatives and early reading and writing programs have proven effective emerge from models developed by theorists working in the area of policy and school change. As is outlined in this book, a literacy-based school change model advocates a strong balanced literacy program that operates within a new infrastructure of administration.

Michael Fullan's involvement with the *National Literacy Strategy* in the United Kingdom serves as an example of improving literacy rates by making changes to the administrative infrastructure of schooling. In an article profiling the success of Britain's program, the *National Literacy Hour*, Fullan attributes the success to six critical elements:

> There are six critical elements to their (i.e., *National Literacy Strategy*) approach: First, set ambitious standards; second, devolve responsibility to the school level; third, provide good student achievement data to schools and provide clear targets; fourth, invest in the professional development of teachers; fifth, establish transparent accountability systems so everyone from administrators to the general public can see how well schools are doing; and finally, intervene in school boards in inverse proportion to success (successful schools and districts take on leadership roles; failing schools and districts receive targeted attention to turn them around).

The *National Literacy Hour* is based on the objectives of offering focus and direction in literacy teaching and learning. Its rationale is to provide a practical structure of time in which to teach literacy. It is set up in this way:

- Begins with 15 minutes of shared text work which represents a balance of reading and writing
- Is followed by 15 minutes of whole-class word and sentence work

Ted Humphries rewrote all of the warning signs and notices that are sometimes necessary in the front hall for school safety in polite and invitational language, and added a display case for copies of letters and notices that the school had received or sent to celebrate authentic literacy. (Do signs asking visitors to report immediately to the front office really keep out intruders?)

- Is followed by 20 minutes of group and independent work with mixed ability groups (some doing guided reading and others completing a writing activity)
- Ends with a whole-class discussion in which the teacher reviews, reflects upon, and consolidates all teaching points

Literacy Framework Model

There are several reading and writing programs spearheaded by theorists in the field of literacy that have proven effective with students in a variety of contexts. Research demonstrates that such frameworks have proven more effective in children's reading comprehension than other reading programs on the market. We have identified two programs that fit this profile: *Success for All* and *The Four Blocks.*

Success for All is a school-wide reading program that incorporates tutoring and family support services along with classroom teaching. The major components of *Success for All* are

- Story-related activities
- Direct instruction in reading comprehension
- Independent reading
- Listening comprehension
- Writing

In this program, students work together to improve strategic reading and comprehension skills. The writing program concentrates on creative writing and responding to literature.

With an emphasis on oral language development, *Success for All* also includes story telling and retelling (STaR), emergent reading, rhyme with reason, shared book experience, and Peabody Language Development kit. The second level of the program emphasizes a balance between phonics and meaning, using both children's literature and stories which have phonetically regular text, along with 50 minutes of shared reading daily. The third level emphasizes cooperative learning.

The Four Blocks program provides several varied opportunities for all children to learn to read and write. It is arranged into four blocks: working with words; self-selected reading; guided reading; and writing. The Four Blocks aims to make each block as multileveled as possible. It provides additional support for children who are struggling, as well as additional challenges for children who are independent readers. At-risk students can be supported by intervention programs while participating fully in the program.

There is no ability grouping in *The Four Blocks* program. The blocks can be scheduled in any pattern to meet the needs of individual classrooms. The structure of the program is as follows:

- *Working with words* — In this block, the children work with the word wall, then they work on the phonetic patterns of high-frequency words for reading and spelling activities.
- *Self-selected reading* — A teacher starts this block by reading aloud. The students then read a self-selected book on their own while the teacher conferences with individual children.

- *Guided reading* — This block aims to give children opportunities with different genres to teach reading comprehension. Whole-class, partner, and small-group formats are used with membership in various formats, changing often to maintain the multilevel methodology. This is the most difficult block to maintain with a mixed-ability group.
- *Writing* — Each day this block starts with a mini-lesson. The teacher then helps students revise, edit, and publish. The writing block is carried out in writer-workshop fashion.

Reflecting on the Process

- What would you and your staff consider to be the "best possible" literacy curriculum you could ever imagine? What resources would you need to support your program?
- What would the students achieve in this "best possible" literacy curriculum? How would the staff facilitate their development?
- How do individual teachers currently establish their timetables in your school?
- What literacy materials are presently used? Do they form the basis for the curriculum or are they seen as isolated resources?
- Are reading, writing, and talking the centre of the curriculum?
- How can the learning achieved by staff members who have taken in-depth professional courses in such areas as writing, children's literature, or drama education be most profitably shared with others?
- How can the staff at your school take ownership of in-school or district-wide workshops to make sure the events are significant to their needs?
- How can you facilitate the attendance of your staff at educational conferences that are coming up to support a new literacy vision?
- What areas of change could you and your staff inititate in trying to institute a new or modified literacy curriculum?

Concluding Thoughts

Although many of the principles and practices foregrounded in this chapter derive from the strength of research and information on the content of literacy education, they have been framed within our overall goal of promoting literacy-based school change.

As a literacy principal, you should understand and be proficient in issues tied to literacy education. There should be a shared vision in your school of what people need to know to organize and manage a comprehensive reading and writing program that includes literacy events across the curriculum and opportunities for development as individuals, as part of small groups, and as part of a literate community.

Schools need teams of teachers to design and implement programs that support each child's development over the years. As lead voice in your school, you create the foundation for building the capacity for a literate community.

Leading for Literacy: Roles of the Leader

Kathryn Broad

Kathy Broad is the Director of the Elementary Initial Teacher Education Program at the Ontario Institute for Studies in Education in the University of Toronto. Her doctoral study explored transformative leadership for school change. Her current research and learning includes teacher induction, teacher development, and school leadership.

In the past five years, there has been an incredible growth in our knowledge and thinking about literacy and about leadership. Conceptions of literacy have broadened and deepened, to include multiple ideas about texts and multiple ways of knowing and being literate. Notions of leadership have also expanded and become more nuanced, emphasizing less formalized and more shared or distributed leadership practice. In my study and experience over this time, I have come to believe even more strongly in the relational nature of leadership for literacy and learning. I see leadership as a complex, interconnected, and dynamic web of approaches and actions that can be somewhat captured in the following framework: leader as learner, teacher, partner, advocate, and researcher.

For me, leadership at its core is about learning. As leaders interested in developing literacy, it's vital for us first to recognize that we must be the lead learners. There has been an explosion in the knowledge base of effective literacy practice — multiliteracies, critical literacy, and information about the processes of reading from cognitive science. All leaders are challenged to keep reading and learning about effective instructional and assessment practices, new theories, and pieces of research, and to re-examine practices in light of these new ideas. At times I've been powerfully confronted with counter-intuitive information about my own methods; for example, realizing that assisting a student too readily or frequently sends a subtle but undermining message about our confidence in the learner that has a direct impact upon efficacy. As well as studying all that research has to offer, as lead learners we must also continue to learn about our own particular context and the strengths, needs, and experiences of our community of learners. We must expect to be surprised and informed by all of the learners in our community.

Implied in this role of leader as learner is an openness to new ideas and understandings, and a willingness to risk and try the unfamiliar. I've come to see the role of leader-as-learner extending into that of researcher or inquirer. Viewing ourselves as inquirers empowers us to take an investigative and constructively critical approach to our work. It allows us to notice things, to hypothesize and to ask key questions: What do our observations and the evidence we have gathered about our learners or practices reveal? What elements in our literacy methods are effective? …surprising? …problematic? What additional information do we need? How can we differentiate for our learners? What are the needs and strengths of our community? Using this approach we can undertake our own inquiry projects, using the evidence we collect to plan and implement strategies and interventions, and then observing the outcomes of those efforts in a continuing cycle of inquiry learning. Questioning often leads to newer and better questions, along with new and different actions and ideas.

The role of leader as teacher — sometimes referred to as "educative leadership" — has also become even more essential. What was once called serving as "instructional leader" has come to mean much more. Knowledge of effective instructional practice and the ability to demonstrate responsive teaching or adaptive expertise — connecting practice to solid research and literacy theory — is critical for leaders. It is also vital to understand and appreciate both student and adult learners, to help everyone to construct their own knowledge and understanding by valuing and building upon prior knowledge and experiences, to ensure that the learning and work are motivating as they are meaningful and connected to the learner, and to keep students as the focus of all efforts. In the role of leader-as-teacher, our modeling learning, risk-taking, and mistake-making become key. We must both "walk the talk" and also "talk the walk," articulating and communicating the rationale for exercising the professional judgement and actions that are the underlying principles, knowledge bases, research, and theoretical underpinnings of our work.

A newer role that I have come to understand and believe in more fully is that of leader as advocate. As we work to transform not only the practices in our schools but also the literacy outcomes for all students, advocacy becomes a central feature. Leaders must be prepared for the fact that undertaking important change may mean discomfort — like living in a house that is being renovated. If we are to focus on literacy, what other elements will be given less attention? What will be our decision screen? In this role, the leader works to purposefully protect and provide precious resources, such as time and person power. This is also where the leader communicates broadly the efforts, successes, and challenges involved in important change and improvement efforts. This is where the leader is able to demonstrate courage and steadfastness in change initiatives. When the inevitable implementation dip occurs, being prepared and ready to maintain the course through a time of unexpected outcomes or disappointing results requires perseverance, strength, and a profound belief in the worth of the undertaking or initiative.

The final role, leader as partner, places collaboration as the foundation of leadership for transformation, particularly in the area of literacy. When formally designated school leaders recognize and utilize the unique contributions and diverse perspectives of all partners — staff, students, parents and community members, colleagues in other schools, district support personnel, federations, governments and universities — capacity for leadership in literacy increases exponentially. This community of leaders, when united in collaborative work on behalf of students, has almost unlimited strength and knowledge as well as capacity for learning and growth. We can ask difficult questions and undertake quite comprehensive change efforts when a diverse and trusting team is in place to consider and offer ideas and share the "heavy lifting." In this way, everyone in the community seeks common understanding, shares energy and power, and takes collective action to support student learning. By understanding and building on the strengths and skills of the community of leaders, the ability of that community to envision, create, and sustain meaningful change is powerfully increased.

Questions that Encourage Learning for Literacy Leaders

Barth (2001) tells us that "learning from experience is not inevitable. It must be intentional" (p. 65). I offer these questions to encourage reflection that can spur all of the many leaders within school communities to learn and grow individually and collectively. The following questions may be used as prompts for thinking, writing, dialogue, or collaborative inquiry among all of the leaders in literacy.

1. What are we most proud of in our literacy programs? What are we most concerned about?
2. What do we want to learn next to improve our literacy instruction?
3. What would we change immediately if we could?
4. What concerns right now hold the greatest potential for change?
5. What kind of collaboration regarding literacy is occurring in our school?
6. What are our current questions about literacy teaching and learning?
7. What issues are coming to our attention? How are they being brought forward?
8. What research information about literacy instruction/assessment/development would be most useful for us right now?
9. Where are our sources of information and/or supports for answering our questions?
10. What prior experiences or knowledge bases am I/are we bringing to bear on this situation/question?
11. What values and actions do I/we want to model?
12. How do I/we select worthwhile projects and protect energy and time?
13. How do we maintain optimism and hope?
14. What does sustainability mean in this context?
15. How does this question or potential project fit with the goals and initiatives of our school? Our system?
16. How are our beliefs and understandings about literacy teaching and learning reflected in our practices and actions?

Play and Literacy

Linda Cameron

Playful Lives, Structured Classrooms

Linda Cameron is an Associate Professor at the Ontario Institute for Studies in Education, where she specializes in Early Years Education. As well, Dr. Cameron speaks internationally as an advocate for the Arts in Education.

For many of us, school experiences were quite different from those experienced by children today. We sat in rows; the teacher stood at the front of the classroom; the blackboard reminded us of what we were working on; and we were silent — *apparently* quiet and well-behaved. But underneath the silence was play — secret codes that careened around the room, private jokes, plans affirmed by nods, gossip and pointed looks, notes passed with fear of being exposed (that was part of the excitement), and other games of wit and wile.

In those days, backpacks were designed for serious treks, not laden daily with burdens of homework. School books were the school's books and stayed there. School time generally contained delivered lessons, drills and worksheets, projects, and one-page compositions. Students that did not finish assignments within the allotted time were envigilated after the final bell tolled — a serious punishment. Time outside of school was precious. Three-thirty, and we filed like silent soldiers down the hall and out of the school to freedom — freedom from adult supervision; the choice of time, place, and direction was ours. We could play!

It was our choice who we would play with, what to play, where to create, what to use, when the game began, what the rules would be, how to protect ourselves, and how to work through our social dilemmas. Supervision and adult interference was minimal. Most kids walked to and from school, collecting or depositing one another as they went: talking, playing, scheming, pretending, exploring, wondering, wandering, fighting and making up, experimenting, dreaming. Ah, the learning that happened en route! The pace (literal and metaphorical) was slow enough that one could absorb the experience with one's senses, develop questions and theories, open up ontological space that could be temporarily superimposed on "reality"— a new imaginatively created reality in which self, objects, relationships, roles, meaning, rules were all redefined. Play was our place, our space, our time to be.

With huge blocks of time, one could develop a story with a plot full of potential, develop a new race, a new world, a new complexity of meaning— a story! Unsupervised, we had to solve the problems and our safety was our own responsibility. We had to keep thinking. Real, robust questions emerged from these adventures, and the inquiry sent the learning quotient straight up. Eleanor Duckworth (1996) defines intelligence as the having of "wonderful ideas." What invites wonder? Exploration. Engagement. Experience. The environment. Conversations. Stories…. Play!

In *Last Child in the Woods* (2006) Louv suggests that kids today are suffering from what he calls "nature deficit disorder" because they lack the multisensory, rich experience of a park, the woods, a brook, or the seashore: places where investigation or meditation are natural, where one can observe life and learn. William Crain, in *Reclaiming Childhood* (2003) suggests that today the thrust is to have children achieve success in the human-made world, thus they develop cognitive skills that enable them to succeed in a high-tech workplace. The development of the child's relationship with the natural world is hardly a national priority. It seems to me that if kids don't experience nature as a friendly, comfortable place of adventure and excitement, they will miss a critical dimension of perception and imagination.

Why Play?

Why this reminiscence? Is it a romantic version of history? No.

We know the importance of the many kinds of play to give voice to the many languages of childhood. Playing school as a means of exploring power and educational concepts, building forts that provide place and space for exploring architectural and mathematical prowess and practical-problem solving — these *were* learning opportunities and a cherished curriculum.

Rich language development is a major byproduct of play. Oral language develops as children negotiate, hypothesize, regulate, explore, interpret, listen, explain, give directions, argue, and express feelings with authentic purpose. As play begins, the initiator enters a temporary ontological space, and any collaborator needs to "buy into" this space. The space may in fact be jointly created or negotiated. Let's make-believe, let's pretend and make ourselves believe for now that this object and situation are really something else. (Sounds a little like a deep comprehension skill doesn't it?) Or, as in the case of games, the player must learn and accept the rules constructed for the game — you can only move this block in this way and that one in that way, or you can only have three tries, etc. This process involves serious meaning co-constructing, the stuff of writing and reading and comprehending and communicating. Play involves serious language development. Is that where we learned much of our language skill? Is that where we honed our cognitive, social, emotional, spiritual, and physical skills?

The value of play is significant. Experience tells us, memories remind us, research supports the pleasure and potential of play. Pause and remember one time when you played. What kinds of significant intellectual, physical, emotional, spiritual, creative, imaginative, inquiring, problem-solving things were part of that scenario? Where were you? Who were you with? Why are you smiling? What did you learn, try out, figure out?

What does all of this have to do with being educational leaders?

Structured Lives, Playful Classrooms

Children live in a very different world today. They are pushed, structured, tested, protected, plugged in, kept indoors, entertained, and forced to comply. They are often sedentary spectators, caught in the consumption net by marketers. Elkind (2007) comments that

> Children in the twenty-first (century) have been transformed from net producers of their own toy and play culture to net consumers of a play culture imposed by adults.

Where is the fun for today's children? Play is gone...missing...held hostage! We are all caught up in striving for excellence, hyper-parenting, educational tested standards, corporate growth, globalization, competing for a high score in the current standards of life, ravaged by the torment to be the best. Toys are marketed to assure that children will learn something. Kids' time is usurped by lessons and their responsibility is to win, to perform, to be the best at everything. Schools are measured. Kids are tested. Homework is escalating. Creativity does not matter. Fun is not an important factor. Inquiry, imagination, and interaction are limited by the constraints of the pursuit of excellence. Everyone is trying so hard to get ready, to be prepared, to pass the test. In fact in *Collateral Damage: How High-Stakes Testing Corrupts America's Schools* (2007), Nichols and Berliner suggest that the pressure on kids, teachers, administrators, and even states has been so great that it is threatening the very purposes, morals, and ideals of our education system.

Have we lost sight of what really matters? Let's imagine a classroom that would have opportunities for play as a fundamental part of the literacy curriculum.

Let's free Play!

The Literacy Initiative at Elms Elementary School
Theresa Licitra

Theresa Licitra is an Assistant Principal at Elms Elementary School in Jackson, New Jersey, where she has maintained literacy achievement through inspired and forward-thinking initiatives.

Choosing an Initiative

As a school-based writing initiative, we chose to embrace, present, and support the philosophy, framework, and approach of the *6+1 Trait Writing Model* to all certified staff in Kindergarten through Grade 5. This directive provided the Elms Staff with ideology, concepts, and strategies in order to readily incorporate the *6+1 Trait* model as part of their daily writing instruction and implementation. This model directly aligns itself with our basal reading series and parallels the online resources available on its website and on supplemental *6+1 Trait* writing sites.

These school-based initiatives directly align themselves, both separately and collectively, to the "Criteria for Power Standards" of the model of DeFour et al. The *6+1 Writing Trait Model* exemplifies all of the attributes of the endurance indicator; the cross-content integration used by teachers through instruction, including components of our differentiated instructional initiative, provides the second component of leverage; meetings in, between, and amongst grade levels provides a platform that enables educators to engage in dialogue which is, according to DeFour, "essential to the next level of instruction." Being proactive in the implementation and targeting of both district- and school-based initiatives enables us to directly and effectively target the keys to assessment for learning: consistency, timeliness, and differentiation.

Implementation

Targeting the first trait, *ideas,* all teachers worked with learners as they developed ideas in their writing. Meetings specific to each grade were attended during the weeks of October, at which time teachers shared writing samples from their classrooms, which had been developed and holistically scored using the *6+1* rubric. These meetings provided time for teachers to focus on the standards, analyze their assessment, and use the information obtained as they reflect on accountability of instruction and student performance. Utilizing this model, the literacy focus was established in the areas of comprehension, expressive written language, and skills development.

Incorporating the *6+1 Trait* model and its five-point rubric, which is in direct alignment with the NJDOE rubric scale, set the premise for the morning's discussion. Data sheets for each classroom teacher, comprised of NJASK scores, end-of-year assessments, and unit test scores, provided a focal point for instruction. All teachers were reflective in the areas of their classes' strengths and targeted areas in need of refinement. Targeted writing traits were *ideas* and *organization; voice* was being introduced. Ms. Roberts noted that voice is a strong component of writing and provided an integral piece to focus on in order to strengthen and influence instruction.

Maintenance of the Program

During the first weeks of December, special education teachers, along with support personnel, met again to reflect and discuss the results demonstrated by the initial baseline student assessments; this data and analysis will continue to be used for instruction. The initiative at the Elms Elementary School continues to focus on a "curriculum by design model, incorporating prioritization and planning" (DuFour 2005) utilizing standards, assessment, and accountability.

A quarterly checkpoint was determined for written responses to a picture prompt and to a poem aligned within the grade-level Literacy Pacing Guide. Holistic scores and student performance on the end-of-unit tests were recorded. Student progress was monitored and students in need of supplemental literacy assistance were identified. The reading teacher provided remediation through small-group instruction and lesson modeling. Supplemental programs such as *Reach for Success* and *Voyager,* and an extended after-care program called *Beyond the Bell,* offered supplemental support to those students identified as being at-risk.

Involving the Community

Throughout, the literacy focus is in the areas of comprehension, expressive written language, and skills development. The message to the Elms educational community that it is important for children to read and to be read to was reinforced through the implementation of the Principal's Buddy Reading Program. Activities that highlight reading — such as Barnes and Noble Night, Read Across America, Book Fairs, and Mystery Readers — continue to motivate learners and strengthen literacy skills.

The Elms Elementary School continued its collaboration with the Jackson Public Library and highlighted summer reading initiatives that learners could pursue with their families at the Jackson Library or through their own independent reading. The Elms Parent Teacher Network, in collaboration with the Elms staff, presented reading incentives to learners at all grade levels. The Jackson Township School District implemented its Summer Reading Program in June 2006, which continued in June 2007, providing learners with both a book and corresponding activities, providing a model that offered titles that were both appealing and grade-appropriate. Assemblies were held and all students were given information and incentives regarding our Summer Reading Program. These initiatives served to foster increased student interest in reading across and within the grade levels.

Tracking Progress

The vice principal and the reading teacher reviewed the district literacy pacing guide and the NJCCCS for each grade level. Model literacy lessons based on the standards implemented by the federal *No Child Left Behind* Act and New Jersey's *Reading First* incentive were demonstrated and modeled by the reading teacher and the vice principal. Exemplary practices using scientifically based research methodologies were implemented and monitored at all grade levels through the checking of plan books, through informal observations, and through formal teacher evaluations.

Ms. Licitra and the reading teacher continued to meet with MLLD teachers, resource teachers, and members of the child study team in order to assist students to meet performance objective and adequate yearly progress. On request, model lessons presented by the vice principal and the reading teacher continued to be demonstrated, with both descriptive and prescriptive feedback developed and exchanged.

Staff development continued its focus: throughout the year educators were provided with opportunities to improve their instructional practice with the *6+1 Trait Model,* providing a common language for both teacher and learner as it prescribed a targeted, focused model of standards-based instruction. Special area teachers collaborated with classroom teachers and devised specific grade level cross-content activities that targeted literacy concepts: Awesome Adjectives and Art; Music and Poetry; and Technology and Literacy. In September 2006, January 2007, and September 2007 (scheduled), the Jackson Township School District In-service Committee, for which the vice principal at Elms Elementary is a committee member, presents their In-service Professional Development to all staff, with differentiated instruction continuing to be a major focus. Differentiated activities continue to be implemented across the content area and, in all grade levels in the upper elementary grades, specifically Grades 3, 4, and 5, literacy and math objectives continue to be the area of intended focus.

Literacy in Middle and Secondary School
Mark Federman

Creating a Vision for Literacy

Several years ago, our English classes were dominated by whole-class novels that many of our students couldn't read, wouldn't read, or pretended to read when asked to read on their own. Emphasis in content areas was totally on content, not on access to text, although most students could not access the text. The bottom line was that most students just would not (and many could not) read the texts in front of them. Students viewed reading as a chore rather than something to enjoy or access as a resource. Consequently, students were spending very little time actually reading, so they were not growing as readers.

Some teachers found success with implementing a small-choice, independent reading program at the beginning of each block. Other teachers and school leaders (including myself), who were a little hesitant about "teaching" fewer whole-class novels, started to see that the students who were given a choice and time were actually reading much more than other students. We discussed and studied this, and made a commitment as a school to explore a school-wide Independent Reading program. First, we committed to spending the first twenty minutes of English blocks (or, as we called them, humanities classes) in Independent Reading, where students could choose any book they wanted to read and would read silently. The teacher would "model" reading by quietly reading in front of the class and make sure that all students were reading (or quietly pretending to read). This was a great start, because kids were actually reading more than ever, and many were enjoying it.

However, we noticed a few problems. First, because teachers' class libraries were not substantial enough, and the school library was a bit antiquated, students did not have choice to the extent they needed. Many of the most interesting or desired books would be grabbed off the shelves. Also, although many students chose books that were interesting to them, often these books were too difficult for them to read. Furthermore, we found that the length of time that the students read was still not enough or was inconsistent. The twenty-minutes-a-day requirement was shorter in some classes and longer in others, and students were not reading as much at home as they needed to, even though some teachers required it. Last, but not least, there was not enough consistent direct involvement or instruction by our teachers to move students to the levels we needed them to be at.

It all became incredibly clear. What our students needed to become truly independent and powerful readers were the following three things:

1. Choice and Access: Students needed easy access to books they wanted to and could read.

Mark Federman is a principal at East Side Community High School, a 6–12th grade public school on the Lower East Side of New York City. Mark has created a strong culture of literacy in his school with consistent literacy achievement over the years.

2. Time: Students needed uninterrupted, uncompromised time to read these books independently in school and at home.
3. Instruction: Teachers needed to teach students through mini-lessons, reading conferences, and other methods how to choose books, how to become more powerful readers, and how to make reading plans so that the students grow as readers.

These three things, along with the professional development, structures, and money to support them, would ensure that our students and teachers found great success and joy. Most importantly, it was my job as principal to make sure this happened.

Implementing a Literacy Initiative

CHOICE AND ACCESS

In today's world of hundreds of cable channels on television, it is rare to find a teenager who would say that there is nothing to watch or no new video game they would like to try. We wanted to have a school where no student ever said, "I am not reading because there is nothing to read." With the insurgence of young adult fiction and texts over the past ten years, there really is a book — in fact, many — for every young person. We set forth to acquire as many of these books as possible.

The expectation immediately became that every English/humanities teacher would have an extensive library in her/his classroom. We shared titles, consulted various professional lists, combed bookstores, and spoke with students to gather the titles we wanted, and then stocked the libraries with these titles. In looking for titles, we focused on books that were of high interest to our students but made sure that the levels varied. We paid particular attention to finding high-interest, low-level books. In addition, we set up each library with attractive, labeled book bins (something that I modeled in my office and will discuss later). This helped students find books more easily, supported them in developing favorite genres and taking risks with newer genres, and made the libraries more attractive in general. The libraries have continued to take off and grow as we regularly replenish them. Each year, we place a minimum of two large orders for which teachers, the librarian, students, and I choose the new titles we want. Also, teachers purchase books throughout the year to replenish the libraries. They are each given a sizeable allotment for which they get reimbursed, and many of the teachers purchase even more books using their own money.

In addition to building classroom libraries, we hired a new librarian from our teaching ranks and revamped and restocked the library. Using funds from our regular budget and through several grants, we ensured that our library had the hottest and latest young adult titles and that we covered all levels and genres. Students have three great places to find books: their classroom, my office, and the school library. Their choices are abundant, and there is always a variety of books in any student's interest at his or her current reading level. If there isn't, the teachers, librarian, and I are always willing to purchase any book that a student requests. Often, we buy books with particular students in mind. There is nothing more empowering for a student or for making a student a powerful reader than when an adult walks up, hands her or him a book, and says, "I saw this book, thought of you, and bought it for my library so you could read it."

As adults, we cherish any quiet moment we can find to escape into a book. We wanted and needed this same opportunity for our students. Once we created the access and choice that students needed and matched students to books, we needed to ensure that students had a sufficient span of quiet time to fall in love with reading and get lost in books. Therefore, we made sure that our school schedule afforded each student, in Grades 6 through 10, 30 minutes of uninterrupted, non-negotiable time for Independent Reading, which grew to 20 minutes a day in Grades 11 and 12. Our hopes were that, once students had this time to fall in love with books, many would actually want to read independently outside of school. Just to make sure, we set the expectation that students would read for 60 minutes a night, and reinforced this through standardized reading records, making the expectation explicit to families and grading students on their home reading.

As a result, you can walk into any English or humanities classroom in our school, on any grade level, during the beginning of class, and find 95% of the students engaged in their books. This is sacred time — if you to dare distract them with anything other than talking about their books, they will not have it. It is common to hear a universal "Awwwwww! Please…a few more minutes?" when the teacher says it is time to put the books away. In addition, almost all of our students are reading regularly at home or somewhere outside of school.

INSTRUCTION

Once we provided students with the choice and the time they needed to fall in love with reading, we realized we needed to provide more direct instruction to help our students become powerful readers. Our teachers needed to be trained in the instruction of reading. Therefore, we attended various professional development sessions and training with the Teachers College Reading and Writing Project, brought in staff developers, and eventually recruited one of our teachers as a full-time literacy coach. Through this professional development, many professional conversations, regular inter-visitations to classrooms, and a commitment to maximizing the results of our literacy program, we took our program to the next level. We strengthened our mini-lessons, articulated and developed the reading strategies we needed to teach our students, modeled strong reading practices through read-alouds, and built strong skills and systems for reading conferences with students. This full-fledged reading workshop allowed us to build a reading program that was heavily student-centered, that created intrinsic motivation, and that naturally differentiated direct instruction of reading strategies, skills, and habits.

Some of the instruction with which we provide students can be broken into three parts:

- matching students to books
- instruction around reading strategies
- increasing their reading levels.

Teachers must know how to match students to books and how to provide instruction that allows students to make independent reading choices that not only suit their interests but also their needs. The more a student is aware of his or her needs as a reader, the more he or she can choose texts that help him or her grow as a reader. We teach students how to know if a book is the appropriate level, and strategies to comprehend and interpret these texts. Teachers support students in making reading plans, where the students make a list of books they would like to read in order of increasing difficulty. That way they have "goal books" (books they want to read but that are too difficult for them to read at that time) toward which they are working and are consciously aiming to increase their reading levels. As students move gradually into more difficult texts, they are taught strategies on how to approach and read more challenging books. It is much easier — and we have seen much evidence for this — to motivate students to become stronger readers because they strive to read a desired book, than to push them to read more because it will help them do better on a test or because reading will make them better readers.

Examining the Role of Leadership

In some ways, it is difficult to separate my roles, because a large part of our success has stemmed from the wonderful collaboration that our staff — of which I am an organic part — demonstrated in developing and embracing this program. However, there are some very important things I did and continue to do, things that seem like common sense but really make a difference.

During my first year as a principal, I decided to wear my message on my sleeve and never apologize for it. I made it explicitly clear to our students, staff, and families that we were going to tackle the literacy issue. I outlined five things in a presentation that I regularly give to other principals:

1. PUT YOUR MONEY WHERE YOUR MOUTH IS

I knew that the type of literacy program my staff and I wanted would require the basic support of the school leadership on several levels. I would need to buy books and build libraries, create a schedule that provided time for reading, and provide our teachers with professional development. However, it would not be enough to just spend money on all of these things; I would need to live them as well. If staff members are sent to professional development (PD), or are provided PD, it changes teachers; if principals and school leaders attend and experience PD with groups of teachers, it changes schools. Therefore, I often attend professional development sessions with teachers and continue to be part of the teachers' ongoing learning regarding the instruction of reading.

2. GET TO KNOW THE STUDENTS AS READERS

This includes getting to know the books they are reading or want to read. I regularly visit classrooms, ask students what they are reading, and speak with them about their books. I hold reading conferences with students and interview them about their reading. I look at their reading records and have done school-wide reading surveys and research on our students' reading. I do book checks to make sure students are bringing home their books or are always carrying their Independent Reading books. I listen to students and utilize them as advisors and consultants on book purchases. I regularly speak with teachers who know young adult books, sharing titles and students' favorites. I browse the *Young Readers, Young Adult,* and *Teen* sections of bookstores and libraries, read young adult book reviews, and check out Hot Pick lists in magazines and online. And most importantly, I read young adult fiction and non-fiction regularly.

3. BUILD A LIBRARY IN YOUR OFFICE

I wanted to make sure that my office was not a place where students were sent when they got in trouble or for other negative circumstances. I wanted it to be a place where students came on their own to celebrate learning, to celebrate reading and books. I also wanted to provide a model and set a standard for what I wanted classroom libraries to look like. Therefore, in my office I built a young-adult library consisting of over 2000 titles. Books are organized in colorful bins by genre, and are easy to access. This is one of a few ways I send a clear message to my students, staff, and families about what is most important in our school. It also helps me ensure that the majority of my interactions and conversations with students are focused on what really matters: reading and learning.

4. START A PRINCIPAL'S BOOK CLUB

The Principal's Book Club started as a response to four issues. First, I was learning about and reading so many great books that I needed a better way to share them and get them in students' hands. Second, I was also trying to figure out more formal ways to establish myself as a model reader and literacy leader. Third, I missed teaching. And last, but not least, I saw many issues cropping up in students' lives.

Every couple of months, I choose five to six titles of mixed genres and levels, purchase 30 to 50 copies of the book, and place a *Principal's Book Club* seal on each book. I conduct a "book talk" with students in their classrooms or at town meetings, or I write a letter to the students introducing the books. The books are then distributed to the different classroom libraries, and any student can sign up to read any Principal's Book Club book. Once the student has read the book, she or he writes me a letter or e-mail and then attends a lunch or meeting to discuss the book. Each book-club book is typically read by anywhere from 40 to 200 students (15% to 40% of our student population).

In choosing the books, I consider books in series (because students will usually read the rest of series); books that are hot off the presses; favorite authors (again, to spur students to read their other books); timely books that fit into a particular season, part of the year, news event, or theme month (e.g., African American, Latino, Women's Heritage); books that have been made into movies about to be released; and important issues that teenagers are grappling with. I would like to address this last category for a moment, because it is one of the most important reasons why we must allow students to choose their own books, and it is one of the best ways we can support teenagers. Today's teens regularly encounter racism, sexism, homophobia, ageism, violence, teen relationships, pregnancy, peer pressure, bullying, divorce, abuse, and many other issues. Yet they often do not have the tools or the models to address or responsibly handle these situations. Adults are often hesitant or do not feel qualified to help students tackle these issues by themselves. Luckily, there are more and more young adult books (fiction and non-fiction) that address these concerns. If we can get these books in our students' hands, they can see responsible models of how young people handle these issues, models we can use as a launching pad for comfortably addressing and exploring these issues. This is called "bibliotherapy." And one of my goals with the Principal's Book Club, and with our reading program in general, is to make sure our students have access to books that will help them become not just better readers but better people.

5. ENGAGE, EDUCATE, EMPOWER, AND INVITE FAMILIES

Extend literacy to the home and beyond. One more role in which I see my leadership as necessary is that of ensuring that families understand the importance of our literacy program for the development of their own children. I start this by making sure that the reading expectations are clear to all families. I communicate this regularly in person and in writing, and I have a PowerPoint presentation, titled *10 Ways You Can Help Your Child Become a Better Reader*, that I present to all families at least once. Furthermore, the students' teachers and I regularly provide them with a complete picture of their son's or daughter's life and growth as a reader. This includes reading records (in class and at home), books read, conference notes, and plans for growing as a reader. Last, but not least, I have regular check-ins with families about how the program is working for them and their children.

6. SPREAD THE LITERACY WORK TO ALL CONTENT AREAS AND TEACHERS

For this piece, I focused primarily on our Independent Reading program, which is implemented by our English and humanities teachers. However, our focus on literacy has spread well beyond these classrooms. Currently, our arts, math, science, and social studies teachers see addressing literacy as a crucial part of their job, both as a means to improve students' reading and writing, and as a way to help students access and understand the content. They participate in professional development and constantly consider the students' literacy needs while planning curricula, instruction, and assessment.

Managing Change

In conclusion, my role as a leader goes well beyond just stamping an approval on the latest reading program or cheering (or barking) from the sidelines. By collaborating with teachers to create the program and by participating in my own way in every aspect and phase, managing change is something that feels natural. The program was developed over time by a group of teachers and leaders who were not satisfied with the results we were getting and who knew our students deserved more. As a result, we actually see this as more of a journey than an actual program, and are open to any and all changes that may help us and it to better serve our students. I must admit that I am fortunate enough to have a brilliant and phenomenal staff that makes this difficult work a bit easier. However, it is crucial for me to never forget that it is my responsibility as a leader to ensure we all reach our full potential.

CHAPTER 3

Creating Literacy Success in Your School

> As principal of the Dramatic Arts Continuing Education courses at our faculty of education, I certainly recognize the need to include literacy-based strategies to help teachers learn with, through, and about the arts. The staff and I work together to plan and develop curricula that can help educators work inside and outside a variety of modes in order to both build community and encourage artful and mindful responses to the texts of our lives.
>
> Larry Swartz, OISE-University of Toronto

Now that we have taken a macro view of the factors necessary for, or at least conducive to, creating literacy-based school change, as well as some of the principles and practices that underlie literacy teaching and learning, we offer some practical strategies for implementing successful literacy initiatives in your school.

A literacy-based school stresses the unity of learning through language. It looks at how children learn and how teaching practices affect their learning. Literacy is a necessary part of all curriculum areas, which in themselves can provide the context for much of the literacy and language use and growth that occurs. Literacy learning takes place naturally and continuously across the curriculum as children approximate, explore, and evaluate. In informative or entertaining contexts, children must see literacy as a source of personal satisfaction.

Language is acquired through use, as those who have learned a second language well understand. Literacy-based teaching strategies grow out of building a curriculum on the way children actually acquire language proficiency — by talking, reading, and writing through need and desire. Whatever the label we give literacy teaching, it can become a metaphor for change — a call to question, examine, and reassess assumptions, and to reflect on what we are doing as educators. Teachers and principals need to engage in dialogue with learners and be open to learning about children, about reading, about writing, and about learning itself. They must also engage in dialogue with one another, observing, coaching, and learning through the creation of a community of professionals, just as in classrooms they strive to create communities of learners.

Teacher education programs are beginning to require personal awareness of and reflection on what makes a good teacher. Teachers must feel they can effect change in the classroom. They must also realize that their own learning does not end when they leave university. They must be ready to explore new approaches to learning, classroom planning, effective practice, and continuous assessment of how children are learning rather than looking at test results. Supportive administrators and colleagues, who share their convictions and work with similar approaches, can help build on successes and failures.

At his school, principal Lorne Browne used to bring his guitar and perform folk songs for a different class each week, incorporating his hobby with school work. As he distributed song sheets to the students, many students read the words as they listened.

Supporting Literacy Success

For most people, reading is a vital part of life, both in their personal lives and in their work. Teachers need to establish environments and reading experiences that can help children develop competence, as well as positive attitudes toward reading. Young children, in particular, must have plenty of opportunities to read and meet with success early in their school years in order to appreciate the value of becoming independent readers. To learn to read, all children need to experience effective models of writing — from computer instructions to history books to adventure novels — and to witness the numerous purposes of reading.

There are several crucial elements necessary for putting in place a sound reading program:

- Ample time for reading, writing, and discussion throughout the day
- An abundance of quality children's literature — fiction and non-fiction
- Guided reading experiences where print is examined with care and precision
- Reading in a variety of groupings and ways (e.g., independent, partner, small-group, whole-group, reading aloud)
- Regular opportunities to read, write, and research onscreen
- Ongoing assessment to determine and advance reading development

The sections that follow and a large part of Chapter 4 provide strategies for making sure these elements are addressed.

A principal colleague always kept an old briefcase in his office full of picture books, and would offer this resource to new substitute teachers who were sent to the school — a welcome beginning to a strange setting.

Bob Copeland is Superintendent of Piscataway Public Schools in New Jersey, and has had significant experience as a teacher, consultant, and administrator.

Speaking About Literacy
Robert L. Copeland

To a principal I'd have to say, "You need some principles. The journey that you're about to take is going to be pretty painful and you have to be willing to lead. Your job isn't to protect teachers from teaching. Your job is to empower them and insist that they use their skills on behalf of the kids."

To a primary teacher: "If you get it done right, life is a lot easier for everyone else. You need a knowledge of the psychology and the science of literacy that probably far exceeds what you've learned in college." We are thinking seriously about requiring our primary teachers to take courses that would lead them to ESL certification, only because the courses you need for that require a really strong depth of knowledge in linguistics.

To the middle- and high-school teacher (and even the intermediate-school teacher), I'd say, "Content matters. You're teaching literature. You've got to read. Sorry, there's just no way around it. It's not sufficient to know what is good writing, you've got to know *why* it's good writing." They have to be well-read people — not only children's literature or the student literature, but also learning in literacy so that they're not learning along with the kids. How do you design lessons to make a kid want to volunteer to come to your class and learn? How do you design instruction, activities that are really gong to engage kids? What's important? Teaching can't be geared to the five kids who sit in the front and think *Beowulf* is a really neat thing to read. How do you get the kid who's staring out the window interested in that piece of literature?

Addressing the Different Interests and Needs of Readers

As has been discussed already, children do not progress at the same rate through the stages of reading. It is the school's job to take all children from where they are and help them progress toward independence. The following are some strategies you may wish to share with teachers in order to address the needs of various types of readers.

STRATEGIES FOR OVERALL READING GROWTH

There are certain strategies that teachers can use to help students become better readers, regardless of where they might be in their reading development. These include

- Basing teaching on a sound theory of how children learn; in particular, how they learn to read
- Selecting texts that children can read successfully on their own and that will make them want to read other texts
- Providing opportunities for children to read increasingly difficult texts
- Encouraging students to reread texts on occasion for the sake of developing fluency, and to read selected texts and parts in order to develop varied responses (e.g., to examine theme, author style, etc.)
- Ensuring that children always read to make meaning and that they find significance in what they read, both on the page and onscreen
- Modeling the use of strategies for growing as a reader, and modeling the use of self-assessment strategies to monitor this growth
- Assisting children in using such techniques as visual information, sound–letter correspondence, analogies, and words within words to advance knowledge about language
- Helping children to connect the processes of reading and writing through cooperative writing activities and through the creation of significant written responses to what they have read
- The use of graphic organizers. There are many resources that provide amazing varieties of organizers for pre-reading, during reading, post-reading, pre-writing, etc. These give students new ways to interact with text, and to record and organize their thinking about texts

STRATEGIES FOR READERS IN DIFFICULTY

Readers in difficulty often require more assistance to achieve growth than children who are progressing as expected through the stages of reading. This can range from additional help in the classroom and at home to the kinds of intervention outlined in Chapter 2. Here is an overview of the necessary supports for this type of reader:

- Programs that stress strategies for growth
- Extensive assistance as they extend their abilities
- Additional one-on-one conferring and demonstrations where needed
- Texts that are predictable and that contain easily discernible patterns (especially for young readers in difficulty)
- Activities to build letter and word patterns
- Opportunities to incorporate new sight words into speech and writing
- Time to respond to reading selections

Ivan Thompson worked as a tutor with an at-risk child every day that he could for fifteen minutes. By the end of the year, he was known by every troubled reader as someone who would help them. In addition, he became very knowledgeable about new and supportive reading strategies.

- Occasions to reread texts, both for pleasure and for the development of fluency
- Encouragement to develop literacy habits such as browsing, reviewing, and selecting to support the development of a personal taste in literature
- Varied opportunities to experience success in reading and bolster their confidence as readers
- Real reasons to read and write both on the page and onscreen

STRATEGIES FOR ESL/ELL STUDENTS

The major obstacle in achieving reading growth for ESL and ELL students is an unfamiliarity with the vocabulary, structure, and patterns of the English language, as well as inexperience with the culture in which the language is used. The following are some strategies that your teachers might find helpful in addressing the needs of ELL readers:

- Pair ESL/ELL readers with buddy readers, preferably other readers who have developed reading ability in English and can foster the reading skills of their partners
- Include plenty of demonstrations for the entire group so that ESL/ELL readers do not feel that they have been singled out
- Include a range of reading materials in the classroom that reflect and honor other cultures
- Provide a range of reading experiences, including shared reading, guided reading, and group read-alouds, so ESL/ELL readers can experiment without a fear of failure
- Find ways to draw on children's knowledge in their first language in learning English
- Tape stories and novels children are reading and make these tapes available to all children so they can use them as needed
- Encourage ESL/ELL readers to complete written responses with a partner or as a member of a small group
- Make ESL/ELL learners aware of response forms that do not rely only on writing, such as drama and visual arts
- Make parents a part of their children's reading program by discussing strategies and goals of the program, and what they can do to help their children read at home
- Encourage ESL/ELL children to get involved in community projects and events that can provide significant opportunities for learning language

Incorporating Assessment

To help you monitor the overall effectiveness of reading programs in your school, we have provided a reading observation schedule on page 87.

In order to design effective reading programs, teachers need to know the progress of individual children, their reading strengths and challenges, the strategies they use, their use of cueing systems, the types of books they want and need, their attitudes toward reading, as well as the strengths and weaknesses of particular teaching methods and programs. Ongoing assessment and evaluation is a necessary component of a strong reading program — so vital, in fact, that we have devoted all of Chapter 4 to the topic.

Barbara Howard invited different children into her office every Friday to share with her the books they were reading. She also read one aloud to them from her own excellent collection located on a shelf she had labeled *The Principal's Bookshelf*.

Reading Observation Schedule

- Are teachers modeling reading through significant and frequent read-aloud sessions, incorporating different types of texts and styles in community-building literacy events?
- Are students reading often throughout the day in all curriculum areas — not just in language arts — using different text forms, both print and electronic?
- Do students have opportunities to read in shared reading situations, in instructional groups, and independently?
- Are students engaging in significant read-aloud events, where students bring words in print to life (e.g., reading scripts in groups, participating in choral speaking and singing, sharing their research and reports)?
- Are students making their own choices about the texts they are reading much of the time?
- Are students keeping a record of their reading choices and experiences?
- Are students reading from a wide variety of materials, including different styles, genres, and formats, as well as being exposed to informational technology?
- Are students aware of different authors and illustrators, and are they developing personal preferences?
- Are students applying literacy strategies as they read, as well as after they have completed a text?
- Are students monitoring and repairing their comprehension as they read?
- Do students have reasons and opportunities for rereading texts?
- Are students responding to what they have read, critically and creatively, using reading journals or through the arts?
- Do students talk with others about what they are reading or about what they have read? Are they reading as "writers?"
- Are students reflecting about what they have read and using their literacy experiences in other ways?
- Do students see themselves as successful readers, growing in confidence and competence?
- Are students beginning to recognize their own growth as readers and set appropriate goals for development?
- Is reading becoming a useful and satisfying lifelong activity for students? Does reading add to the quality of their lives at home and at school?

Building a Culture of Literacy

It is not enough to address just the strategies necessary for individual growth as readers. Principals also need to encourage teachers to establish a reading community with the whole class. By doing so, children have the opportunity to

- Participate in the ongoing literacy life of the classroom
- Come to value reading in a more global way
- Begin to support one another in developing the attitudes and strategies required as lifelong readers/writers
- Benefit from teachers as models of literacy as they share the kinds of literacy activities in which they believe

At Huron Heights Secondary School, with the support of an excellent administrative staff, two teachers in the English program have created a digital literacy course for the students in Grade 10. All course outlines are online; students submit all projects electronically; the dialogue journals between students and their teachers are onscreen; blogs and chatlines are in place for student interactions; and the independent projects in which the students are engaged are worked on in the library, which is well-equipped with print and electronic resources, with teachers and library staff for the students to confer with one-on-one. During our visit to the school and in our interviews with staff and students, we observed an exciting and meaningful educational environment, with everyone we met participating in literacy events using technology as a means of supporting and encouraging growth in young readers and writers.

Later that day, we attended a staff meeting run by a team of teachers; the meeting covered an extensive agenda involving reports from groups of teachers about the different activities carried on throughout the year, including programs for Grade 8 students from neighboring feeder schools and strong remedial literacy courses for at-risk students. It was evident from the number of projects involving staff and students that this school was an educational community committed to the best for their students, with literacy as a core component of every program.

For more on the Walk-Through process, see Principals as Role Models by Susan Schwartz on page 104, and The Principal's Walkabout by Gwen McCutcheon on page 109.

The Walk-Through Process

Susan Schwartz

I participated in a session with a board last week called the Walk-Through Process. We walked into 20 classrooms and, in three minutes, we could see what was going on in terms of the cognitive approaches of teachers, the participation level of the students and the instructional strategies. It trained us to really use our eyes and to look at the rooms to see what the kids were doing, to see what the teachers were doing, and be able to understand the expectations that the teachers have of kids. We could actually get an overview of what was going on in each classroom in three minutes. The whole process was an attempt to get teachers and principals to become more aware.

As an administrator in a high school, I walked into a class and the teacher stopped me at the door and said, "What are you doing here?" I replied, "I am just here to visit. I am in classrooms all the time. I want to find out about the curriculum." But she was uncomfortable with my being there, and this meant that I had to go back to that department and ask for help. I want to be in classrooms; I want to know what is going on; but some teachers may feel that I am there to evaluate them — I know that I am there to learn. School is about creating a culture together.

Creating Writing Opportunities

Writing activities in classrooms can essentially be divided into three major categories:

1. *Independent writing projects* — regular opportunities for students to work independently on topics they usually select for themselves
2. *Research inquiry* — drawn from the curriculum, although at times teachers may assign a topic from a theme or genre the class is exploring as a community
3. *Guided writing instruction* — done with a group of writers gathered together temporarily to work on target areas of writing techniques and strategies, such as conventions, genre study, or technological skills

To help you monitor the overall effectiveness of the writing programs in your school, we have provided a writing observation schedule on page 91.

Whatever the activity, there are a couple of significant strategies that teachers can use to help students improve their writing skills. First, connecting writing activities to the reading process where possible helps strengthen overall literacy development. When writing and reading are combined, children have the opportunity to put into practice their awareness of how print works. Second, allowing students to write about topics and issues that matter to them as much as possible provides motivation for acquiring new writing skills.

An open and accepting writing environment in a classroom is essential and should offer a range of writing experiences and products. These might include such forms as diaries, journals, letters, surveys, how-to-do books, games, resumés, bibliographies, autobiographies, lyrics, poems, articles, editorials, essays, memos, advertisements, commercials, brochures, questionnaires, petitions, dialogues, screenplays, and legends, to name a few.

Consider the Writing Process

Students need to realize that writing by definition is recursive: writers consider ideas, write drafts, revise, find more information, edit what has been written, share drafts, reorganize what has been written, edit again, consider published models that interest them, and sometimes even give up and start on another project. Much of writing is personal, meant only for a writer's eyes. This writing is seldom edited. Other writing is meant to be communicated, and students need to understand that these pieces require further consideration before publishing.

By rereading their own writing both silently and out loud, as well as conferencing with peers and the teacher, students can develop the ability to see changes they want and need to make in their writing as they refine their first drafts. It is essential to help teachers understand that revising and editing are important and essential processes for students to undertake when preparing pieces of writing for publication. Many students realize the need for editing, but have difficulty revising their ideas and changing the structure of their writing. When examining early drafts, teachers need to look beyond spelling and grammar errors in their initial conversations with young writers and help them look at the bigger picture.

In assisting your teachers to effectively implement the writing process in their classrooms, you may wish to consider some of the following strategies:

- Plan ways with the staff for them to model the writing process for their students. By sharing their own writing and reasons for writing, students can learn about the different aspects of the writing process from teachers. For example, a teacher could demonstrate strategies for revision by writing in draft form on the blackboard or on an overhead transparency.

- Decide as a staff what parts of speech or aspects of syntax teachers could focus on over the course of a year at each grade level, and brainstorm games or explorations that could help children discover how language works.
- Encourage staff to follow up on activities in various curriculum areas with collaborative group writing. For example, a group could write a summary of a science experiment, prepare a chart illustrating a concept learned in social studies, or write a poem in response to a drama lesson.
- Promote the use of journals as a means for students to reflect on significant events from their lives, the books they have read, and ideas for future writing. Although they may choose to keep parts of their journals private, they can be encouraged to select pieces for response from their teacher.
- Write a letter to parents encouraging them to respond to content and ideas in their children's writing and to help them with the revision process where appropriate. You may wish to hold an evening meeting to share techniques for helping students in different stages of the writing process.

Focus on Spelling

Learning to spell is clearly related to students' general language development. Students go through developmental stages in learning to spell, but not necessarily sequentially or at the same rate. Spelling is not just memorization; it involves processes of discovery, categorization, and generalization.

Spelling is a thinking process. Students learn the patterns, regularities, and unique features of spelling as they read, write, play with, and attend to words. To help students grow as spellers, teachers need to draw students' attention to specific patterns or groups of words to help them see rules or generalizations. Struggling spellers need to focus on a small amount of information at a time, especially in examining connections among words and word families, and can benefit from such strategies as mnemonic tricks.

Students need to attend to the appearance of words and to check their encoding attempts. As they try to spell words, they often discover the underlying rules of the spelling system. More experienced spellers fix up their misspellings as they go along, correcting those words they already know, rather than waiting until they have finished writing. Students can benefit from learning how to do these quick checks, heightening their ability to know when a word looks right.

Before teachers tell students how to spell words, they need to ask "What do you know about this word?" and build on students' knowledge. For example, students can be encouraged to circle words in doubt. When they return to the words, they can write them over until they look correct. By considering a pattern or generalization that applies, or saying a word slowly and stretching out the sounds, students can learn to picture words "in their mind."

To assist your teachers in helping their students to become better spellers, you may wish to consider some of the following strategies:

- Provide opportunities for staff to acquire further background in spelling in order to help their students apply patterns and generalizations in spelling new words.

David Booth enjoyed reading the school newsletters from his son's elementary school. The principal approached the task so creatively, including children as columnists, parent views, and community news from student reporters. The principal's own comments, which were always in his personal voice, were delightfully engaging.

"Linking spelling with reading has a two-fold benefit. The words students meet in reading provide words for study. It is not just the content of the stories that makes reading and reading instruction useful, it is also the development of reading skills and strategies that can be used in other subject areas. As students have more experiences with print, they build a bank of knowledge about words."
— Clare Kosnick (1998)

- Find ways to share the latest spelling research. For example, a group of teachers could read a significant article, and then report on and discuss information with the rest of the staff.
- Suggest to teachers that, as a staff, they create a file of strategies and ideas drawn from or inspired by various books and articles on spelling and punctuation, to help them cope with problems individual children are having with writing words.
- Encourage staff to use spelling texts as helpful resources rather than as a complete program. Some published programs are developmental and permit student choice and can therefore help guide the learning and monitoring of student progress.
- Share relevant spelling research with your school's parents and explain how the school is assessing and monitoring children's spelling development. Suggest meaningful ways for parents to support their children's spelling growth at home.

Writing Observation Schedule

- Are teachers sharing examples of quality writing models with the children (e.g., letters, stories, folklore, non-fiction, samples of student writing, samples of their own writing)?
- Are students engaged in writing activities several times throughout the day?
- Do students write about what matters to them and for authentic purposes?
- Are students writing in different genres and formats?
- Are students recording their personal reflections and feelings, as well as sharing ideas and experiences for future writing projects?
- Are students involved in the writing process — selecting a topic that matters to them, composing a first draft, and then revising their work?
- Are students editing their final drafts carefully, using references and suggestions from peers and the teacher?
- Are students sharing their writing projects through classroom publishing and presentations?
- Do students treat research projects as writing opportunities, and follow the stages of the writing process?
- Do students draw from their experiences in reading texts as resources for writing?
- Are students becoming more aware of the craft of writing, noticing techniques authors use and trying them out in their own writing?
- Are students becoming aware of the need of writing for an audience, in other words, learning to write as "readers"?
- Do students participate in opportunities for instruction, such as personal conferences, interactive writing sessions, and sessions for sharing their writing?
- Are students growing in their knowledge of how words work: keeping a personal spelling list, exploring common principles and patterns of spelling, learning more about punctuation and usage?
- Do students have opportunities to use the computer for different writing functions, such as word processing, revising, editing, formatting, and doing information searches?

Technology Infusion: From the Outside In

As technology advances, so do our literacy practices to respond to them. Certainly, as a result of technology, there are different sorts of literacy practices employed today than there were twenty years ago. Practices like word processing, web searches, scanning documents, and even pointing-and-clicking and cutting-and-pasting are now fundamental to the writing process.

In response to this, as principals, you need to assist teachers in incorporating technology into their literacy programs. To support the students in developing technology-related skills, the literacy curriculum should include the following teaching strategies:

- Use the Internet as an instructional resource and for online learning programs
- Develop web navigation strategies with students
- Have the students use the Internet to support research and writing
- Ensure students make full use of word-processing features when publishing pieces of writing
- Encourage students to enhance their writing through fonts, color, spreadsheets, graphs, and photos
- Have students share pieces of writing with other young writers on the Internet
- Allow time for students to foster relationships with readers and writers around the world through e-mail
- Encourage various forms of electronic communication through e-mail, mailing lists, and newsgroups
- Incorporate CD-ROMs, videotapes, and films in literacy programs so that students can access different forms of information
- Have students listen to audio books

Supporting a Whole-School Approach to Literacy

See The School Community: A District Approach by Cathy Costello on page 101.

As has been discussed throughout this book, literacy initiatives in schools are most effective if there is a whole-school commitment to creating literacy-based school change. To create a culture of change means establishing a commitment to change and a community of teachers that advocates literacy improvement. This includes not only manifesting changes in classroom space and daily routines, but adopting a new perspective on roles and responsibilities.

As a literacy principal, there are a number of ways you can promote a whole-school approach to literacy. Although most of these have been touched on already, this list provides a summary of the most important considerations.

- Review all literacy programs in the school with the staff and commit to continued improvement, planning, and professional development with a school literacy team
- Encourage teachers to constantly reflect upon and share ideas in order to plan instruction, as well as to monitor, track, assess, and reflect upon student development in all areas of literacy
- Offer preparation time and professional development for staff in developing, planning, and organizing literacy initiatives

- Put in place appropriate resource personnel, such as staff leaders or a literacy coordinator, to serve as coaches, mentors, and partners for your teachers
- Make sure timetables reflect a schoolwide priority for literacy by providing extensive time blocks in each class focused on reading and writing
- Explore flexible timetables that allow for each of the following in classrooms:
  - time for teachers to read to students
  - a daily silent-reading time when students select their own books
  - opportunities for group reading and interactive response
  - book talks by teachers, students, librarians, and/or visitors
  - rehearsed oral reading by the students for real purposes such as readers theatre or reading buddies
  - reading conferences that allow teachers to observe the reading strategies individual students are using and to assess the meaning they are making as they read
  - the integration of what students read with their writing
  - time to engage in different aspects of the writing process
  - attention to how words work, such as word families, patterns, and core vocabulary
- Provide assistance for at-risk students in the form of remedial support or second-language acquisition support where needed, as well as the chance to work in flexible groupings and settings with other students to reinforce particular knowledge and skills
- Ensure that all classrooms are organized for a combination of large-group, small-group, and individual literacy activities at all times
- Promote print-rich environments in each classroom and throughout the school in the form of classroom libraries; references, such as dictionaries and thesauruses; word lists and walls; writing rubrics; experience chart stories; information charts; samples of students' writing; banners, and signs; notices; computer resources; etc.
- Support the creation of classrooms where students are immersed in a world of words through listening, speaking, reading, and writing in a variety of ways
- Encourage an examination of a variety of media, such as television, radio, newspapers, and the Internet, to foster literacy development
- Suggest that writing activities be connected to the reading process often so that students recognize the reciprocity of the processes of reading and writing
- Promote literacy events across the curriculum so that students see that reading and writing cross curriculum borders and that literacy is integral to all subject areas
- Foster communication and cooperation with parents throughout the school year about their children's literacy development, accepting their concerns, sharing with them significant observations and data, and valuing their support at home and at school in building lifelong learners

Dear Jayshree,

Whenever I spend time in your classroom and observe your interactions with the students, I regret that I cannot spend more time with educators like you. You bring literacy alive by offering your students authentic and meaningful language events.

As a literacy teacher, you respond to student needs when they arise and you engage children in your classroom. By encouraging students like Rashid to predict meaning in stories, you provide them with myriad strategies they can draw on when they face new literacy challenges.

Based on Monday's observation, you generate lively discussions and connect stories to the children's own experiences. Your discussion as a prelude to the story about Japanese immigrants was an apt segue into a story about emigrating to a new country. In particular, I admire the way you connected the story to your own experience so that students appreciate that you, too, know what it feels like to be inducted into a new, foreign culture.

Upon entering your classroom, I was immediately struck by the fusillade of environmental print, posters of authors, and children's work as responses to texts read in class. Having said that, given the number of English as a Second Language students you have in your class, you may want to locate some more multi-ethnic texts for your classroom library. In an effort to create an inclusive culture, I am encouraging our staff to use the halls and walls as a reflection of our community and, indeed, to promote the efficacy of cultural diversity in our school. Incorporating authors and their writings from our students' host cultures reinforces the fact that we bring our heritage to bear on our interpretation and depiction of texts.

Jayshree, your teaching is intensive and responsive. You know how to help growing readers like Kieran feel at ease with their progress. However, you may need to place more emphasis on the different cueing systems, as I noted that some readers like Marika relied only on phonics cues to guide their reading of the story. Marika sounded out four words over the course of her reading of the short passage and you did not respond in any of those instances.

Your level of engagement, enthusiasm, and organization comes out in everything you do and say. By acknowledging strategies students use in their literacy pursuits (e.g., noticing first letters, searching for meaning in pictures, reading left to right with eyes, and recognizing frequently encountered words) you give students greater confidence in their reading and writing. Do let me know if there is anything I can do to help you in your teaching and learning.

With respect,
David

Learning Communities

Support networks often involve the comprehensive system a school develops to help beginning teachers or experienced teachers new to a school adjust to a school's culture, administrative requirements, and expectations. As Susan Schwartz explains, support networks can also create "collaborative vision" in a school. Here, Schwartz offers an example of "collaborative vision" in a school in which teachers share their expertise:

In a school I visited recently, a principal had an elaborate sharing system with teachers whereby six or seven teachers worked together for a block of time when they delivered programs to different groups of students.

In addition to in-school support, teachers also require professional support from outside the school if literacy-based school change is to be effective.

This chart outlines some of the conditions necessary for providing support to teachers at several levels.

Inside the School	Outside the School	Across a Larger Network
Set a culture for change and a desire to improve	Cultivate community involvement	Create collaborative networks for teachers by grade level and interest
Offer administrative support and leadership	Share information about successful programs	Provide sources of new information
Free up time for professional development	Ensure you have adequate supplies and materials	Provide opportunities for visitors and guest speakers
Provide effective and inviting work spaces and reading resources	Find personnel and resources to support professional development	Consult outside sources and professional materials for up-to-date guidelines on running and implementing programs
Exhibit professional materials (e.g., articles, books, etc.)	Provide training and ongoing support through outside professional development	Be receptive to research projects by districts and colleges

School-Based Educational Specialists

School-based resource personnel are often key to the success of literacy-based school change. These specialists may have various functions, including

- Working in one school over time so they know the staff, administrators, and students
- Continuing to teach students over time, thereby basing professional development on the particular needs of a school
- Being released from the classroom to develop and implement a professional development system that is integrated and meets a school's vision
- Having an ongoing relationship with a school, and even being a part of the parent community
- Working closely with parents and having a stake in school achievement
- Gathering data, thereby contributing to research in a given area and reporting back findings to a school

The following are descriptions of specific in-school roles that principals may wish to consider incorporating as a part of an overall school literacy plan:

- *The instructional team* — These people are selected by the principal from a pool of volunteers. They set agendas for weekly meetings where teachers share ideas, discuss curriculum, and ask the group to help them with specific students.
- *Peer mentors or coaches* — In this role, master teachers and less-experienced teachers with expertise in a specific area, such as language arts, are paired with first-year teachers. They can also collaborate with more-experienced colleagues who request assistance while implementing a new strategy.
- *Resource teachers* — These people are specialists in areas of the curriculum and provide positive learning experiences for mainstream teachers. These specialist teachers can work with teachers during lunch and/or during planning periods before or after school.
- *Literacy coordinators/coaches* — As a resident expert of literacy education in a school, a literacy coordinator provides in-school support for teachers as they develop and improve their instructional and assessment skills. Part of the job includes assisting teachers in implementing strategies for grouping students and solving literacy-related problems with staff. Such a resource person shares his or her knowledge and expertise with teachers and engages with parents as partners in a whole-school commitment to literacy success. As well, a literacy coordinator organizes and maintains literacy resources for teachers, including professional materials that can supplement current knowledge of literacy teaching and learning.
- *Literacy committee* — This group consists of the principal, teachers, and often parent representatives. It provides support in the form of meetings, plans long-term events and activities, and even handles some budget concerns.
- *Administrators as instructional leaders* — The primary aim of administrators as instructional leaders is supporting teachers by responding to questions and providing resources they will need to do their jobs.

District-Based Educational Specialists

Teachers often benefit from the assistance of outside resource personnel in their efforts to create literacy-based programs. These people may perform a number of functions, including

- Working at the district office and spending considerable time in schools — this allows for an understanding of the school system, including such factors as politics, community, past problems, etc.
- Providing professional development for teachers at a range of schools and across grade levels
- Providing support for teacher educators working at a school-based level
- Working with administrators at a range of schools across a district so they are aware of district-wide trends, patterns, and initiatives
- Specializing in a grade level, which allows for the development of a broader expertise in providing professional development in many settings

Dr. Lyn Sharratt is the Superintendent of Curriculum and Instructional Services for York Region District School Board. In 2002, under the strategic leadership of Director Bill Hogarth, Lyn developed her vision of moving students' literacy achievement forward with a structure known as the Literacy Collaborative; this initiative became a way of bringing school teams together to deepen their knowledge and understanding of effective literacy instruction.

Lessons in Leading for Literacy

Lyn Sharratt

1. A school district must involve all layers of leadership in being focused, knowledgeable, and aligned. You cannot align the district to your focus on literacy and your intention to improve literacy achievement if you leave out field superintendents working with principals.

2. It is crucial to use data to arrive at a focusing question for the work of schools, at both an area level and a school level. There may be areas in a school board where schools demonstrate common patterns of achievement or lack of achievement; data will help to focus attention on areas that require more intense and knowledgeable efforts. Similarly, at the school level, data will help to determine specific grades, groups, or even approaches that will become the work of teachers in that school.

3. There are those who say, "Don't do too much too quickly." However, I have learned that it is far better to "go full-steam ahead" with all the early adopters you can find. In that way, you can build enthusiasm and create a core of knowledgeable literacy experts whose zeal can infect the teachers with whom they work on a daily basis.

4. It is absolutely essential to include special education teachers all the way along. They already have a key role in supporting language acquisition and literacy skill development, and act as advocates for those students who struggle or who have special needs. They need to be key leaders in understanding the system vision, too, while implementing strong instructional strategies in literacy with every staff member in every school.

5. Intensive support of some schools may be required. You can provide a healthy measure of ongoing professional learning for all schools, with more support going to some that really need extra assistance.

6. Differentiation of instruction, resources, support, and professional learning is very important.

7. It is necessary to reflect on why you are doing what you're doing, so that you spend money wisely. Critical friends are important to evaluate efforts and to keep them real. Action research or teacher inquiry is pivotal in helping you move from "me" to "we." Having an inquiry question to focus and guide the instructional plan in the classroom then allows you to share the discoveries and results with others. It's all about caring for those children beyond your own classroom, school, and district.

8. Hold your nerve! You will encounter nay-sayers along the way, especially two or three years into implementation when others might think that priorities should be changed. If literacy is the crucial skill for the 21st century, then you must find the sticking point and stand your ground.

The following are specific outside roles that can benefit a school in the process of creating literacy-based school change:

- *District consultants* — Many districts hire educators to act as consultants or specialists in particular curriculum areas. These people usually work with individual teachers or groups of teachers within a school or groups of teachers from across the district to provide assistance with programming or offer professional development related to particular needs.
- *Private consultants* — Private consultants work on a "cost for service" basis and generally have a high level of expertise through constant work in many schools. These consultants often bring fresh ideas from the outside, as they work independently for a professional-development company or publisher. They often have access to new materials and can visit your school to organize such events as teacher-organized study groups, informal lunch meetings, and consultant-facilitated study groups.
- *University-based teacher educators* — These consultants work at a university or college with whom a school may have a partnership. They can provide fresh, new ideas from outside the school and are often knowledgeable about new research and instructional strategies. They may assist in curriculum development, do field-based research in a school to contribute to the field of education, or work in partnership with a school to offer seminars and workshops. Student teachers and their advisors participate in practicum sessions in specific schools which adds support to the regular program.

Community Cultures

Although research has shown that it can be challenging in some districts to elicit parental involvement and interest in literacy initiatives, it is well worth the effort to include parents at a variety of levels. Once parents are presented with concrete ideas for getting involved, they often rise to the challenge and serve as important partners in the literacy process.

Parents are a child's first and most important teachers. Parents who read for their own interest, read aloud to their children, and talk with their children about reading and writing, promote literacy by conveying that reading is an important, and normal, activity. Schools should make determined efforts to encourage and broaden parents' reading with their children.

Keeping in touch with the home through interviews, conversation, reports, and cooperative projects is now common practice. Many schools send home a monthly newsletter to inform parents about the upcoming month's assemblies, fundraising efforts, excursions, birthdays, and other celebrations.

In Lucy Calkins and Lydia Bellino's *Raising Lifelong Learners: A Parent's Guide*, they explore the role of parents in supporting children in their literacy pursuits. At one point in the book, Calkins and Bellino speak of supporting early attempts at literacy behavior:

> To support children's early progress toward reading, it is helpful to anticipate, watch for, and celebrate the progress they make en route to being independent readers. To do this, we must realize from the start that children often "pretend" their way toward being readers. The child who holds a book upside down and "reads" an elaborate fairy tale is on his way toward reading.

As part of our pre-service school partnerships, we work with a principal who has created a reading tutorial program where student teachers get to work with a reading buddy for a half hour every day they are at the school. Together each child and student teacher write a summary report at the end of the five-week session that is sent home to the parents, describing and celebrating the literacy growth of their child.

An accompanying calendar often highlights classroom and school events. Parents have responded enthusiastically to this type of monthly correspondence as it helps them to plan and to discuss what goes on in school with their child. Teachers who take the time to prepare these letters/calendars feel that they form a significant bridge between school and home.

As lead voices of literacy-based school change, principals must demonstrate to parents how children learn language and develop as language users. Difficulties can arise when parents do not know about the school's philosophy of literacy teaching. Teachers need to constantly inform parents about the strategies they are using and provide careful documentation of each child's growth. Parents need to understand how literacy is the basis of the curriculum, so that when they see their children reading silently and aloud, revising, explaining, and researching, they will know that their children are learning about language as they work with it.

When parents hear children read aloud chorally, see them create a poetry anthology, or receive from them handwritten invitations to classroom events, they will recognize language learning and literacy growth. When parents help in the classroom, taking part as storytellers, scribes, or assistant librarians, they will see children involved in real literacy experiences. When parents see teachers' plans — with long-range goals set out — and observe careful records of children's progress, they will grant teachers the support they need to make a curriculum based on children's own language development success.

Effective school leaders recognize the strengths of a solid relationship with the community in building significant literacy programs. The following are some strategies your school might want to try to get parents more involved in a whole-school literacy commitment:

- Encourage parents to read to or with their children each day
- Compose a letter to parents inviting them to recommend books that they have enjoyed reading with their children to share with all parents
- Plan ways to involve parent volunteers in the library to shelve books, review new materials, and read with children
- Institute a schoolwide program where parents can assist children who are having reading difficulty on a one-to-one basis
- Use parents as researchers by involving them in drawing up questionnaires, holding interviews, and analyzing results and reactions

Families are the primary literacy resource for their children.
- All families should be given support in their important role of initiating and maintaining their children's literacy.
- Once we take into account the cultural and linguistic complexities of family life, the ways of knowing, and the funds of knowledge that families share, we can no longer assume that living in a low-income community means that a mother or father cannot read and write.

— Denny Taylor (1997)

Concluding Thoughts

Classrooms and schools are communities of interdependent people who meet daily throughout the year for the betterment of all. Administrators and their literacy teams need to take the time to discuss such sweeping issues as

- What is literacy?
- Is there consistency in our literacy programs?
- How are we using data and strategies to change programming to better meet the needs of students?

Alongside wrestling with the large issues around literacy teaching and learning, principals and teachers need to work out problems, celebrate special events, and encourage student and parent cooperation and involvement at all times. This highlights the fact that ultimately everyone is responsible for contributing to literate classrooms and schools. Conditions for literacy are as important as the methodologies used to teach it.

This chapter set out to provide strategies for supporting growth in both the content of literacy and the creation of a culture of change. It is really only a start in becoming aware of the processes necessary for effective literacy-based school change to take place. By embracing the experiences and ideas of others, as well as conducting their own classroom inquiries, it is possible for teachers to modify and extend their methods for assisting young readers and writers. It is your job as a literacy principal to set the stage for this to happen.

Reflecting on Literacy Initiatives in Your School

- How does each teacher organize his or her classroom for learning in terms of traffic patterns, materials, furniture, etc? Could changes be made to make the environment more conducive to literacy learning and student ownership?
- In what ways could you increase access to learning materials for your staff that are appropriate to the development of literacy, useful at various work centres, and related to classroom themes?
- How might you work with staff to ensure that multiple copies of textbooks or trade books in various curriculum areas are effective resources and correspond to the school's overall literacy goals?
- How can you help teachers to reflect on their own teaching methods, taking into account their strengths, weaknesses, and biases?
- How can teachers begin to integrate the language processes of reading, writing, listening, and speaking in all areas of the curriculum?
- How might you modify or change the intervention programs currently in place in the school for at-risk readers?
- How might you assist teachers in accommodating children with special needs in regular classroom programs?
- Does your school subscribe to professional resources that can add to teachers' overall understanding of literacy and aid in their practice?
- Is there a framework in place for teachers to share ideas about curriculum and classroom organization?
- In what ways can you help the wider community recognize the holistic needs of children so that you can gain support for your attempts to build a literacy-based school?

The School Community: A District Approach
Cathy Costello

Cathy Costello was the Curriculum Coordinator for Literacy in York Region District School Board, one of the largest school districts in Ontario. Cathy participated on Ministry of Education provincial writing teams for adolescent literacy resources. She is a well-known presenter on topics related to literacy at international conferences.

"The most powerful feature of schools, in terms of developing children as readers and writers, is the quality of classroom instruction. Effective schools are simply schools where there are more classrooms where high quality reading and writing instruction is regularly available. No school with mediocre classroom instruction ever became effective just by adding a high-quality remedial or resource room program."

Richard Allington, *What Really Matters for Struggling Readers*

York Region District School Board (north of Toronto, Ontario) began a journey toward improved literacy achievement in 2002 with a vision, a priority, and a definition. The vision that all students could learn, and especially achieve better results in literacy, came out of the Board's attempts over the previous four years to provide greater equity and fairness in resources and instructional approaches to assist students in schools that struggled to achieve results. York Region is a large school board in a rapidly growing district. It has more than 150 elementary schools and 30 secondary schools. The population is diverse both socio-economically and culturally, with more than 100 different languages spoken by families with children in its schools.

York Region designated literacy as the priority of the Board, and worked hard among various groups to arrive at a definition of literacy that would be forward-looking and do justice to the new literacies of a new century. In the York Region District School Board, literacy is defined this way:

the development of a continuum of skills, knowledge and attitudes that prepare all our learners for life in a changing world community.

- It begins with the fundamental acquisition of skills in reading, writing, listening, speaking, viewing, representing, responding and mathematics.
- It becomes the ability to understand, think, apply and communicate effectively in all subject and program areas in a variety of ways and for a variety of purposes.

Research pointed clearly to the crucial role of the classroom teacher and knowledgeable, skilled classroom instruction in helping children become proficient readers and writers. To increase the number of teachers who were skilled in literacy pedagogy, Dr. Lyn Sharratt, Superintendent of Curriculum and Instructional Services, envisioned what she called a Literacy Collaborative that would build school learning communities focused on improved literacy instruction. In its first three years, the Literacy Collaborative was an invitational activity. School teams, each consisting of a principal, designated literacy teacher, and special education teacher, committed to learning about literacy and learning about change at ongoing professional development sessions at the system level, throughout the school year. Between 2003 and 2004, more and more schools committed to joining the Literacy Collaborative, and finally, in 2005, supervisory officers decided that all the remaining schools would be included in this professional learning initiative by allocating staffing, from existing budget, for embedded Literacy Teachers in every school.

The Literacy Collaborative is built around four shared beliefs and understandings that derive from the work of Peter Hill and Carmel Crevola (1998):

1. *All* students can achieve high standards given sufficient time and support.
2. All teachers can teach to high standards given the right conditions and assistance.
3. High expectations and early and ongoing intervention are essential.
4. Teachers need to be able to articulate what they do and why they teach the way they do (be theory- and evidence-based rather than trade-based).

The goals of the Literacy Collaborative are to increase students' literacy achievement by using assessment data for instruction and selection of resources; building teacher and administrator capacity in literacy instruction; and establishing sustainable, collaborative professional learning communities within and among schools across the district.

In the first three years of the Literacy Collaborative, schools were asked to make the following commitments:

- maintaining literacy as the school focus in the School Plan for Continuous Improvement (SPCI)
- maintaining a Core Literacy Team comprised of at least an administrator, literacy teacher, ESL teacher, and core subject representatives focusing on school improvement in literacy
- ensuring professional dialogue and professional development focus on literacy development for all students
- ensuring literacy development across the curriculum
- setting rigorous performance standards and associated targets that seek to have all students performing at a high standard
- focusing on data-driven instruction/decision making, and diagnostic/formative assessment on a regular basis throughout the year on a full range of measures for instruction
- using data to evaluate the impact of school improvement upon student performance and achievement

Critical friends from the Ontario Institute for Studies in Education (OISE) were invited to be teaching and learning partners in the Literacy Collaborative. Drs. Michael Fullan and Carol Rolheiser were especially instrumental, along with Dr. Lyn Sharratt, in leading the school teams through three sessions per year in change management, productive instructional approaches, and literacy knowledge.

Research conducted by the OISE partners and York Region resulted in a paper (Sharratt and Fullan, 2005) that set some clearer directions and commitments for the work of the Literacy Collaborative. In a close analysis of the results in nine elementary schools, Sharratt and Fullan discovered the "diamonds in the details." Those schools that had committed to and followed 13 parameters produced the best achievement results in literacy. The parameters have been adapted to include secondary schools and now form the basic commitments from every school principal and literacy team of the Literacy Collaborative:

1. Shared beliefs and understandings among all staff (see four dimensions above).
2. A designated staff member for literacy (i.e., an embedded literacy teacher) who works alongside the classroom teacher modeling/demonstrating/coaching successful literacy practices.
3. Daily sustained, focused literacy instruction: timetabled literacy blocks in elementary schools, cross-curricular literacy instruction in secondary schools.
4. The principal as the literacy leader in the school, with a clear commitment to participating in regional literacy in-service and to the ongoing collection and use of individual student, classroom, school, and district literacy achievement data.
5. Early and ongoing intervention in response to emerging student needs across grades/panels. Literacy-rich Kindergarten programs and Reading Recovery™ are examples of powerful early intervention strategies.
6. A case-management approach to monitoring student progress, using consistent classroom and system assessment tools such as PM Benchmarks, the Diagnostic Reading Assessment, exemplars, and other formative, or assessment *for* learning, approaches. Using a tracking wall for students within a division is a helpful case-management strategy.
7. Job-embedded professional learning in literacy, including school-based learning teams to integrate and reinforce sound assessment and instructional methods.
8. In-school grade/division/course or subject meetings focused on developing a shared understanding of standards among staff.
9. Shared literacy resources located in a designated area of the school, including literacy resources materials appropriate to the students' instructional needs. At intermediate and secondary level, where there is an emphasis on subject textbooks, this approach includes the use of text sets or alternative rich resources to provide students with other avenues to discover, understand, and learn the knowledge of the subject.
10. Commitment of school budget to acquiring literacy resources that are current, inclusive (respectful of student's cultural background, gender, and unique academic, social, emotional, and linguistic strengths and needs), and of high quality.
11. Staff commitment to literacy learning and professional development; e.g., through action research/teacher inquiry, book study, professional reading.
12. Parental/community involvement in supporting literacy, through family reading nights, borrow-a-book programs, parental instruction in reading with their children, Ontario Skills Passport, etc.
13. Appropriate literacy instruction in all areas of the curriculum where teachers plan for and provide literacy instruction related to the subjects they teach.

To widen the sphere of learning and involvement, a number of other pieces have been included in the Literacy Collaborative over five years:

- Literacy Content Training in literacy and mathematical literacy has been provided from the beginning for divisional teacher teams from each school through a series of professional learning days.

- Literacy Walk-Through training has been offered to school administrators as an opportunity to learn the technique of non-judgmental observation and reflective conversation with individual teachers in order to support the building of a learning community.
- Intensive Support Schools have been selected for school-based support for 1/2 day per week by a consultant who works directly with a designated literacy teacher and the school administrator to extend school-wide capacity for improved student achievement in literacy.
- Literacy@School has linked teachers through online portals to literacy demonstration classes located across the Board that are designed to support teachers in their continued understanding of successful instructional practices in literacy and assessment for all learners.
- Action research or teacher inquiry involves teachers in some schools in designing literacy instructional approaches and gathering data on their practices.

In addition, each school is accountable for reporting on its journey at a Literacy Learning Fair held in June of each year. At this event, schools are arranged strategically in groups of three to share their year's literacy learning and achievement — their successes, their challenges, and their next steps for the coming school year. The Literacy Learning Fair is a true celebration, providing lessons about literacy accomplishments and change management strategies that are transforming York Region District's schools.

Richard Elmore, in his research on effective professional learning (2005), indicates that a culture of professional accountability is achieved through

- high alignment/coherence among responsibility, expectations, and accountability;
- high alignment of practice;
- high transparency of practice;
- high support that is focused and individualized as needed; and
- high agency — an attitude that says, "If I can't do it, they'll help me do it. If we can't do it, we will learn together."

York Region District School Board has moved strategically toward those alignments with its Literacy Collaborative. While York Region has been growing by at least five schools annually through the years of the Literacy Collaborative, and the population has become increasingly diverse both culturally and socio-economically, district results on all the Provincial EQAO assessments have improved in each year. It appears that the focus on improvement through intentional efforts at the district and school levels provided by work in the Literacy Collaborative is working...but never finished.

Principals as Role Models
Susan Schwartz

I strongly believe that leaders in schools need to be role models for literacy. For example, Shelley Harwayne, school administrator (principal, superintendent) and author of a number of professional books for educators, is a true literacy leade; she models her love of literacy and what she expects from teachers, stu-

Susan Schwartz is a former principal, currently working at OISE/University of Toronto in the Master of Teaching Program and in the new 5-year Concurrent Teacher Education Program. She is the co-author of several books for teachers.

dents, and her school community and district. She is my role model. She "walks the talk" and continuously demonstrates her strong commitment to literacy. Much of what I describe below reminds me of her.

Making Resources Accessible

When I was a principal and vice-principal (nine years in four schools), the first thing I did was set up my office to reflect my love of literacy — complete with many picture books and professional resources to lend to staff, students, and parents. On the walls, I posted pictures highlighting diversity and inspirational quotes that encouraged reflection. My puppet collection was a hit, as was my apple collection and other interesting objects that encouraged questioning and wonder. I remember one day a new student to my school whispered to her mother, "Mommy, look. It's a library!" In the early years of my principalship, when female principals were not the norm, I was often mistaken for the librarian. I felt rewarded, however, when someone borrowed a book from my office, or initiated conversation about one of my resources. It was actually a good way to begin the process of finding out about my students and their families, or finding out about the teachers' interests, program, and practice. I believe that principals need to lead by example, to maintain their own professional library as well as develop one for their staff.

I also displayed picture books and left resources in the staffroom for teachers and parents to browse and borrow. I made sure that the picture books were powerful ones that highlighted diversity, social justice, and multiple perspectives: such as *Encounter* (Voyager Books, 1992) by Jane Yolen, a story told by a native boy watching Christopher Columbus' ship arrive; and *Fly Away Home* (Houghton Mifflin, 1991) by Eve Bunting, a sensitive story about a homeless boy and his father who are forced to live at the airport. Today I might use books such as *My Name is Yoon* (Farrar, Straus & Giroux, 2003) by Helen Recorvits, or *My Name is Hussein* (Boyds Mills Press, 2004) by Hristo Kyuchukov, or *My Name is Bilal* (Boyds Mills Press, 2005) by Asma Mobin-Uddin and Barbara Kiwak, all powerful books highlighting diversity and social issues. I ensured that the librarian had a large section in the library for novel sets and current teacher resources, including a huge area for professional books and articles about early literacy, English language learners, assessment and evaluation, etc.; also prominent was a section for parents to sign out articles, brochures, and professional resources. It warmed my heart to see parents taking out materials to find out more about education and how to help their children. Today, I know that many schools have entire literacy rooms for parents, ones that I hope are clearly accessible and inviting.

Reading Aloud

Another thing that I did often as a role model for literacy was read aloud to my students, staff, and parents. My love of picture books was clear when, on many occasions, I shared different books with my community. I remember, in my first year in the principal role, the School Council meeting when the parents met me for the first time. There were about 20 parents in attendance and, instead of talking about myself, I read aloud a picture book called *A Children's Chorus* (Dutton Children's Books, 1989) by UNICEF, which shared ten rights of children. In making connections to this book, I talked about my philosophy and goals for my students and school community. I think I pleasantly surprised the parents and certainly made the point that my top priority was my students and that literacy was a focus. During my first week as principal in this school and in my next elementary school, I went from class to class, reading aloud to the students. One of my favorite books was *Chrysanthemum* (HarperCollins, 1991) by Kevin Henkes, about a little mouse who becomes the victim of name-calling. With students in Kindergarten to Grade 6, I was able, during the discussion that followed this read-aloud, to make some important points about name-calling, bullying, safe schools, and respect. I continued to read aloud at all student and parent assemblies and open houses, targeting the phrase, "There is a picture book for every occasion."

As a role model and curriculum/literacy leader, I also read aloud at staff meetings, and often shared ideas and resources. When I was vice-principal for a year in a secondary school, I once read aloud to a group of about 40 high-school teacher-leaders. I think they were taken aback by my choice of a primary book called *Fortunately, Unfortunately* (Aladdin Books, 1993) by Remy Charlip. However, using the pattern in this humorous book, I was able to share some negative information that encouraged looking at the positive. Picture books became a catalyst, leading to discussion and questioning where everyone was encouraged to voice their views.

Celebrating Literacy

I strongly believe in celebrating teaching and learning. Celebrations and community get-togethers in my schools included parent information nights, open houses, family literacy nights (where children and parents come together for in-service on how to help children at home), literacy weeks, authors' festivals, author/illustrator/poet of the month, and whole-school or individual-classroom sharing. I invited the community in — had fathers come in as role models, as well as male and female police officers and fire fighters. Reading and sharing together became a community responsibility. Knowing how important it is for children to present for an audience, I encouraged many celebrations. These required planning and organization, but were well worth the effort, as writing and student work were highlighted and praised, increasing self-esteem and pride in student accomplishments. This was performance-based assessment at its best, providing concrete evidence of student learning and teacher success.

Focusing on Authorship

I believe that creating a school culture that embraces literacy should include a focus on writing and authorship. Writing and publishing (going public) in many forms and formats permeates every subject area and demands competence in skills for everyday life. I think, because of the many changes in education over the past decade — new curriculum documents, many expectations, the standardized report card, etc. — this focus on authorship has been somewhat lost. I believe that emphasizing the writing and publishing process each year in every classroom and in every school creates a sense of authorship and audience, and builds self-esteem, confidence, and self-efficacy. When students are encouraged to write for different and genuine audiences — the director, the principal, the mayor, a pen pal — and for real purposes, writing is made more personal and important. When children and adults feel like authors, they learn about and understand their own writing process, their strengths and areas that need improvement. When teachers are writers, they understand the writing process and are sensitive to what they can expect from their students. They and their students become motivated to write more often and more effectively.

A focus on writing and authorship encourages studying of diverse authors, poets, and illustrators, and this goes hand-in-hand with reading and a focus on talk. Critical literacy is important here; principals and teachers encouraging in-depth questioning and discussion. Difficult questions are asked about differing perspectives, about whose voice is missing and/or marginalized, about personal underlying assumptions. Deep learning occurs when assumptions are challenged and when teachers and students are able to see and respect multiple points of views.

Walking Through

When walking through teachers' classrooms and throughout the school, I want to see evidence of literacy everywhere: reading, writing, media in various forms and formats as exemplars — in student journals, as student-published books, using technology, on bulletin boards, and as three-dimensional displays. One can tell many things about a school and classroom focus on literacy by what is posted on walls and on display. I know that many principals keep a checklist of what to look for in a classroom, so that they can support teachers in their growth in specific literacy areas. Many new teachers need this support and mentoring. Such a checklist can serve as a talking point when preparing for the teacher performance appraisal process, which can become less stressful for teachers and administrators when there are concrete areas to explore together.

I believe that administrators need to be keenly aware of what is going on in each classroom. The Walk-Through process, in which I enthusiastically participated to hone my observation and reflective skills, originated with Carolyn Downey in the 1990s. This practice helps principals find out what is going on in classrooms — teacher use of cognitive approaches and instructional strategies, and the participation level of students. More importantly, it provides administrators with strategies for building trust and strong relationships with teachers. My good friend, Bev Freedman, former superintendent in the Durham District School Board, is currently completing her doctoral studies in this area, and she provides teams of educators with Walk-Through training in many districts across Canada and the United States. Her research and professional development are well worth exploring.

Assessment and Evaluation

I believe another important goal for all curriculum/literacy leaders would be to focus on effective assessment and evaluation practices. All teachers should be assessment-literate, using assessment hand-in-hand with instruction. Teachers are encouraged to use a variety of assessment practices to document and showcase evidence of learning. Self-assessment and reflection are important practices in encouraging students and teachers to become more reflective. As a curriculum leader and role model, I would share with my staff and students my professional portfolios, along with other assessment samples, and invite a focus on self-assessment, goal-setting, and reflection. The use of electronic portfolios would also be a good way to increase reflective practice and skill with the use of technology in thought-provoking and creative ways.

Creating a Collaborative School Culture

As a principal and curriculum/literacy leader, my goal is to increase teacher capacity and create exemplary teachers, teacher mentors, and leaders. When teachers feel supported, they experience success and see evidence of student learning. They feel valued and rewarded, and become more confident and ready to take on leadership roles. With each successive positive leadership experience, interacting with and supporting others in group situations, they gain self-esteem and self-efficacy.

When I first started teaching, it never entered my mind that I would someday be a principal. With each leadership opportunity I experienced, my teaching skills, confidence, and leadership skills grew. Today, more and more teacher candidates are entering their pre-service program with a leadership role as a goal. As a result, they are looking for opportunities to experience leadership and to hone their interpersonal skills. Relational leadership, where leaders "lead from behind," supporting others and group goals, is preferable to the "follow-me" type of leadership. Developing teacher leaders means looking for opportunities to guide teachers into leadership roles, providing them with experiences that will enhance their skills in relating to others, as well as supporting their interests and needs. A good picture book I often use to talk about leadership is *The Tower* (Simon & Schuster, 2001) by Richard Paul Evans. It is about a young man who, in his quest to be great, constructs a tall tower so that everyone looks up to him. By the end of this story, he learns from an old woman that "to be great is not to be higher than another, but to lift another higher." This is an example of relational leadership at its best, and it is a goal to which I strive and try to model.

Creating teacher and parent literacy committees within the school, as well as appointing a literacy teacher leader (even if it is not a paid position), can be beneficial to the increase of effective literacy programming within the school. Looking carefully at school improvement plans and literacy outcomes, and creating a concrete plan of action, moves literacy forward and involves everyone in positive ways.

Creating a collaborative school culture involves building leadership within a staff and with the students and parent community; it means being that role model who sets a positive example for growth and learning. I want my staff, students, and community to know that I am not perfect, but a risk-taker and a learner. It is important to me that they know that, as educators, we are working with the best interests of the students and school in mind. This creates a more supportive attitude within all stakeholders, where all are working collaboratively, striving toward similar goals. When a principal continuously models a love of literacy in the principal role, with literacy as a strong focus, a domino effect occurs, with positive benefits for all.

The Principal's Walkabout

Gwen McCutcheon

Gwen McCutcheon has been a principal with the Waterloo Region District School Board for five years. As well, she teaches a Ministry of Education Literacy Course for teachers.

When I walk through my school, I am looking at literacy as more than a subject, more than the accumulated knowledge and skills that add up to proficiency as a reader and writer. Literacy is the pulse of the school, the energy that drives the critical conversations between student and teacher, student and text, student and student. So, what are the markers of that energy? How do I know the juice is "turned on"? My observations really centre on three basic questions:

- Have we developed a community of learners?
- Have we provided for a balanced program, based upon assessment of student needs?
- Have we the created the opportunity for authentic conversations about text?

Developing a Community of Learners

The teachers commit time and energy at the beginning of the year to create a sense of community in the classroom. Through discussion and class meetings, they establish the norms for the group early in the year. Respect and trust are fundamental prerequisites for risk-taking and learning to occur. The teachers guide the students in considering what respect "looks like, feels, like, sounds like." The class decides on respectful procedures for encountering visitors to the school, new class members, and guest teachers. For instance, in one classroom, the students elected an orientation committee for welcoming new students throughout the year. Respect agreements, a kind of classroom constitution, are collaboratively formulated, written, signed, and displayed. These agreements are on display by Meet the Teacher night so that parents are aware of our values and are part of the conversation.

As principal, I remind teachers that the mighty curriculum can stand and wait while these essential conversations occur in September. What looks like a slow start now will enable rich learning to occur later on. What the principal attends to sends a powerful message about what is important in learning. The teachers and I go on the hunt for respectful behaviors to describe and to publicly celebrate.

Teachers need their own community of learners. As I walk through the school before classes begin, I overhear teachers talking about their pedagogy, their challenges and successes. It is important for the principal to celebrate the spirit of collaboration and to build opportunities into the timetable for professional dialogue to occur. Sometimes that means hosting assemblies or bringing in guest speakers for the children while the teachers meet to plan. I am discovering, however, that the teachers don't like to miss the learning and discussing that the kids are doing in the gym (and I shouldn't be surprised at that!). A better structure is to pair the kids for Learning Buddies on a weekly basis, so that primary and junior teachers can alternatively meet as a group while their buddy teacher manages both classes.

I dropped into Kristan's Grade 5 class and discovered the children in the middle of a lively conversation. Kristan was guiding them through a critical literacy discussion about the text of a song, "Mr. Mom." In the song, a goofy father takes on the parenting tasks traditionally handled by the mother, with disastrous results. Students were challenging the assumptions implied in the lyrics, and making connections to their personal lives and to other media depictions of dads. One child was speaking at length and with passion about how wonderful her father is as the sole parent in their home. Students were turned in their desks to look at her and were attentive to her comments. When the student was finished, Kristan explained to me that the class had been responding to this musical text since yesterday and that I didn't have the full context of the discussion. She then called on Jimmy to summarize the comments made by Lucy the previous day. Without pausing, the boy accurately paraphrased the argument put forth by the girl in the earlier lesson. Lucy confirmed that Jimmy had conveyed the important points she had expressed. As principal, I realized that I was witnessing the full flower of Kristan's culture of respect in the classroom. Those fifth-graders are truly a community of learners who expect to listen and learn from each other.

Creating a Balanced Program Based on Student Needs

SCHEDULING

Creating a balanced program begins with timetabling. As much as possible, the principal and teachers work to create large uninterrupted blocks of time for literacy instruction. Then, throughout the year, every interruption or special event that presents itself to the school must be evaluated rigorously. Is this worthwhile enough to disrupt the deep learning that is occurring in our literacy blocks?

RESOURCES

In my visits to classrooms, I look for a balance in resources. Are there appropriate texts for teacher read-aloud, shared reading, guided reading, and independent reading? Are many genres represented? Some students are keen to read only non-fiction books; others like to stick to a series of books by a favorite author; others like graphic stories or how-to books. Teachers need to make sure that all types of books are available for independent reading, but also must plan to include some of the less popular or unknown genres in their planned read-alouds.

For self-selected or independent reading, it is important to think about how the resources will be introduced and "marketed" to the students. Are the same books piled up in the same bins in April as they were in September? It is better to have a somewhat smaller collection that changes over the year than to set up an entire library at the outset. It is better still to invite the kids to interact with the collection in a dynamic way, choosing to sort the books by their own criteria.

One time I came upon a huge heap of books in a classroom and a group of student excitedly sorting them and talking about them. The teacher had given them the task of organizing all the books into categories of their choosing and labeling the bins. A month later, the students decided that the agreed-upon way of cataloging the books wasn't working and they went through the whole process again. In this classroom, the library is not a static collection, but a changeable feast!

INSTRUCTION

In my visits to classrooms, I look for a balance in instructional format. Are students engaged in whole-group, small-group, partner, and individual work? I am interested in the reasons teachers choose a particular format for instruction in a particular context. Teachers have many different and valid reasons for the instructional choices they make; through my conversations with them I deepen my own learning. The principal can play a positive role in increasing teacher reflection by engaging teachers in dialogue about the instructional decisions that they make on an ongoing basis.

I look for instructional displays that summarize learning and provide direction for future tasks. "Anchor charts" collaboratively developed by the students and teacher are much more valuable than commercially purchased bulletin-board displays. In one classroom, students have produced a list of text features for non-fiction books; in another, there is a chart about what a "good story" has. The charts and instructional displays are often created during shared reading or shared writing lessons, and children refer to them as they embark on independent assignments.

ASSESSMENT

Teachers engage in multiple forms of ongoing formative assessment. They are comfortable with tools such as running records, and use the information to plan lessons. They realize that the greatest power to be derived from data collection is to inform instruction. For many of us, this process is a new and challenging one, and thus best tackled as a team.

> In our primary division, we decided to use the reading data to identify two students in each class who were not progressing well, children we thought we could move ahead with some focused teaching. In our divisional meetings we described the students' reading behaviors, identified their text level, and, as a group, discussed next steps for those students. Throughout the year we revisited and updated the data several times, using a data wall as a visual record. Our discussions got deeper and more specific as we contemplated the reading strategies each student needed and the particular challenges of each text level. We became a bit like doctors, coming together as a group to ponder particularly challenging case studies.

STRUGGLING STUDENTS

As a team we need to think carefully about multiple entry points and multiple "safety nets" for students who are not meeting with success. By early- to mid-Grade 1 we are looking for students who are not learning how to read and we provide them with focused intervention. The district allocates some of our Special Education resource time for this purpose. With children who are struggling, we work from the premise that they need a more deliberate and intensive exposure to the *same* learning opportunities as the other children. We do not fall into the trap of simplifying the reading process for them by focusing on one or two features, such as letter–sound correspondence. Struggling students need the richness of the full program *and* deliberate, focused instruction that enables them to access all the reading strategies. For this reason, we work hard to make sure that the students who work in small groups with the resource teacher do not miss their regular literacy block with the classroom teacher. We are also striving for the same higher-thinking responses that we want of all students. That means we are not satisfied merely with the acquisition of sight words or the ability to read aloud grade-level text. Deeper meaning-making is the goal for all students.

Nancy had been concerned about the prospect of teaching an autistic child in her Grade 1 class. At the beginning of the year this youngster, Tim, demonstrated limited communication skills and very little interest in classroom conversation. However, with the help of an Educational Assistant, Nancy forged ahead, teaching him the Grade 1 curriculum along with the rest of the students. It became apparent that Tim had a good visual memory and was able to master most of the sight vocabulary and many Word Wall words with little difficulty. As a result he could "read" beginning text with success, although with limited response. Nancy continued to include him in small-group guided-reading sessions, where he heard other children making connections between stories and their lives and between text and other experiences. Tim started to mimic these statements in the group sessions, often repeating exactly what other students had said. The breakthrough came late in the year when Nancy was reading one-on-one with Tim. She had provided him with a text written by the same author as a story the students had previously encountered. Tim studied the cover carefully and announced, "There's Brian, the boy who was in the other story. I wonder if his friend James is in the book too!" Nancy couldn't wait to get to the staffroom to talk about Tim's text-to-text connection. Throughout the year, her goals for this student did not differ from her goals for all her students; namely, the development of comprehension and meaning-making. Tim was not withdrawn from the rich classroom discussions to practice rote skills. And despite his severe challenges, he began to understand what literacy really means and how he can be a successful participant.

For students with diagnosed learning disabilities, the current technology is a life-saver. In my walkabouts I see students working on small keyboards beside classmates who are writing; I see students who are using text-to-speech software and special computers that read, write, and produce text for the student; I see one very gifted child using a graphic organizer on the computer to help her create order and a hierarchy out of the encyclopedic knowledge that is in her head. We understand that literacy is the site where thinking occurs and that any technology that helps children get closer to the act of engaged thinking is to be welcomed. For parents who are concerned that their child might be labeled "different," we tell them that this is truly a brave new world where children do not blink an eye at one another's particular learning needs or accommodations.

Mario arrived from another school in May and was placed in Nicola's Grade 2 class. He immediately let his teacher know that he didn't like reading and was not interested in any of the books she was offering. His running-record text level showed that he was performing at a mid-Grade 1 level. Conversations with Mario's mother revealed that, while the family spoke English at home, English was not the first language for either parent. Mario's mother was concerned that he had lost interest and confidence in school. Nicola went back to the running-record data and sat down with Mario. She carefully pointed out all the things he was doing right as a reader and celebrated the learning he had accomplished so far. She provided him with a number of texts that she knew he could be successful with, and enlisted the aid of his mother to read them at home. All the time, she was deliberate in her intent to make Mario feel like a valued and appreciated addition to the classroom community. The next time she called Mario to read with her individually, he was not quite so resistant. Then, one day, Nicola burst into the staffroom and stated, "I know what the problem is with Mario! He doesn't understand the vocabulary!" In the lesson that day, Mario had begun to interrupt the read-aloud repeatedly to ask what a particular word meant. Nicola discovered that his listening comprehension of the English language was severely limited, and that Mario had been concealing the deficit until that point. Our first step was to celebrate Mario as a risk-taker and a learner, and to let the other students know that his attempts to clarify meaning and understand vocabulary were the mark of an excellent thinker. The next step for Nicola was to put in place some focused strategies to help Mario accelerate his understanding of English. She enlisted the aid of the English Language Learning teacher, and built in more read-aloud and discussion time on a one-to-one or small-group basis for Mario. She taught him strategies for inferring meaning from context and checking with other sources. Mario has some work ahead of him, but he is on his way. His teacher's careful attention to learning data and her willingness to let it shape her instruction — as well as her attention to the emotional underpinnings of learning — is what is making a difference for this child. As teachers we need to remember that a child who is behind his peers in reading is almost always deeply worried about that. What looks like attitude, is often dismay and profound fear. Such children need careful instruction in the strategies they are lacking so that they can begin to independently solve text on their own.

Authentic Conversations about Text

The more serious we are as committed literacy educators, the more we run the risk of forgetting the role of student engagement in reading success. Children have been known to leap grade levels to read a text that appeals to them. In my walkabouts as principal, I look for students who can't be pulled away from their books and teachers who are talking all the time about the stories they love.

As teachers and principals, we need to remember to ask the kids, "What are you reading these days?" and to bring in our own reading material from home to talk about. When we are on yard duty we need to remind ourselves to ask kids about their favorite magazines, books, computer games, and movies. In this way we let the kids know that part of "real life" is talking about our experiences with literacy and that their text choices are as worthwhile as the text choices we make for them in school.

In my walkabouts I look for classrooms where literacy is embedded in real objects and real experiences. I walk into Euen's classroom and see tadpoles in a tank; into Ginny's and see caterpillars in cocoons; into Shane's and see an ant farm. These experiences offer rich opportunity for students to listen, talk, read, and write.

Teaching Grade 5 and 6 is an opportunity for Sheila to create authentic social studies learning. Her students spend the year in role as sailors on a ship bound for the New World in the year 1534. They begin the year by applying, in role as young men and women from Europe, for a position on the sailing vessel. The classroom is adorned with sails (white bed sheets hung from the ceiling in big loops) as the group makes its journey across the Atlantic. When they arrive at the Americas, one group goes south and encounters the indigenous Aztec and Inca nations; the other goes north and meets Native Canadian peoples (in this way, Sheila deftly meets the demands of the curriculum in a double grade). The "sailors" keep elaborate and detailed journals of their encounter and report back to one another on ship. The anecdotes in the stories from the Grade 5 students included information of Mayan, Aztec, and Incan life, as they wrote about games they played, people they met, food they ate, and religious rites they witnessed — the boys particularly enjoyed writing about the human sacrifice. The Grade 6 students related how they traveled across North America and the experiences they had with aboriginal peoples: riding in a dugout canoe; tasting corn, pumpkin, and maple syrup; learning to fish with spears; sleeping in a longhouse or teepee; hunting buffalo; etc. Both grades used information from their social studies (Mesoamericans; Aboriginal peoples) and science units (Grade 5: weather; the human body, in the description of skeletal remains found. Grade 6: diversity of living things, in describing the plant and animal life they saw as they traveled; space, in reading the stars as they crossed the ocean or found their direction).

As principal, I invite parents to be part of the literacy dialogue. Parents want their children to succeed and are often searching for the best way they can support the work of the school. In the past, we have sometimes thrown the crusts of the literacy loaf to parents, getting them to work at home on sight-word lists or spelling words, while we keep the deep and significant work for ourselves at school. This year we opened our Home Reading program with an information night for parents. We talked about the "big picture learning" that we were seeking from all our literacy work. We invited the parents to examine the achievement chart on which we base our assessment. They were surprised to learn that text level and reading speed are not even mentioned, and that reasoning, thinking, and comprehending are the focus. We shared strategies that we use to deepen children's thinking around text. We invited them to apply some of the strategies to their read-aloud time with their children and to talk with them about the ideas in the books. We helped them make the important distinction between the little leveled books we were providing for student practice, and the longer, more complex texts we were encouraging them to read aloud to their children. Throughout the year, the children kept a Home Reading journal, recording every night with their parents as they read and listened to stories. Parents wrote notes too, often sharing their experiences with the books they were reading aloud. Initially they asked us to provide lists of good read-aloud selections, but quickly started recommending and sharing their own favorites among themselves. Of course, not every parent loves every book, and differing views emerged, which led to more dialogue. Periodically we held assemblies at school to honor students who had read for a benchmark number of nights (50, 100, 150, 200). By the last assembly, parents were in attendance to cheer and applaud their children's success.

Every time a celebration happens at school, it can be linked to literacy. The graduating class can be encouraged to decide on a favorite picture book and buy a copy for the library. Every assembly can include a brief book talk related to the topic of the assembly and/or to new resources available to the students.

In one classroom, the teacher set up a home reading program and told the kids she was going to try to "catch them" reading in the evening. Over the course of the winter months she made random calls to the children's homes, the way radio announcers sometimes call listeners. She would ask the child what he or she was doing, and if the child said, "reading," the teacher would invite the student to retell some of the story or read a passage over the phone. The following morning in class, the teacher would announce that the child had been "caught reading" and would present a wrapped book gift to the lucky winner. With the support of parents, sooner or later everyone was caught reading! A wonderful benefit for the teacher was the opportunity to hear children read text in their home language. When this occurred, she encouraged the child to bring the book to school the following day to read and explain to the class. The children learned that literacy is honored in all cultures.

The hallways of the school present rich "real estate" opportunities for the development of literacy. The most engaging types of student writing are posted there so that children can read and reread each other's work. One class posts a daily joke, with a lift-up flap for the answer. In Christine's class, each child writes about a favorite book and displays the recommendation along with a photocopy of the book's cover. One of our most successful practices has been the Family Bulletin Board, an idea that we adapted from Shelley Harwayne. The bulletin board is a huge community conversation in written form arising from a question, such as "How did you get your name?" Students work at home with their parents on a bulletin-board submission that may include a brief story and photo. Teachers, custodians, administrators, and office staff are also invited to contribute their story. The display grows as each contribution is added. When the bulletin board is full of written material and photos, it becomes a reading text for the entire student body. The morning announcements can include questions: *Whose name means "beautiful sunrise"? Who was named after a grandfather who loved to tell jokes?* Students can be found lingering around the bulletin board on their way out for recess, trying to find the answer to these "comprehension questions"! Some of the other prompts we have enjoyed include "How do you celebrate?" (focusing on different holiday traditions) and "Who do you love to read with?" (this often elicits beautiful photographs of grandparents with their grandchildren). We have discovered that personal and family stories are powerful impetus for reading, writing, and talking.

My predecessor, a much-beloved principal, was known for his interest in hockey, and would often chat with students about how their season was going; once in a while, he would even show up at the arena when a student was playing a key game. For this he was well-known and well-remembered in the community, even long after he had retired. As for me, I am a polite and supportive listener when the kids talk to me about hockey, but they know that my real passion is literacy. So I show up at the arena of their reading. I read their Home Reading journals once a week and reply to their observations and reading responses. If they write that they love a certain book I don't know, I ask them to lend it to me so I can read it. If their teachers remark on a wonderful story they have written or a poem they have published, I make sure they share it with me. The kids know that the principal does the book buying, so I sometimes go into the classroom with the publishers' sample books, asking the kids to review them for me and make some recommendations. On one occasion mid-year, there was an opportunity to buy a few more books for classroom reading. I already knew what the teachers wanted, so I took only those catalogues into the library and invited the ten most avid readers from Grade 1 (who mysteriously all happened to be boys). These "reading consultants" spent an hour poring over the catalogues, reading the sample books and carefully recording a wish list of titles.

All this doesn't take as much time as it sounds, but I feel it is important. We simply cannot ask kids to put their full energy into literacy unless we do too!

CHAPTER 4

Assessing from the Inside Out

We are well into a new era where innovative societies are not only sustained by a limitless supply of ideas and imagination, but also by the ability to comprehend, compute, and convey them. Literacy facilitates all of these activities and, in turn, fosters a nation's standard of living and quality of life. It is the great enabler.

Frank McKenna, Deputy Chairman, TD Bank Financial Group

"Principals need to understand assessment in a variety of ways. I think principals need to be really effective models of assessment portfolios and reflective practice, demonstrating to teachers that effective assessment can happen with everyone in a school, especially if the principal is modeling the process all the time."—Susan Schwartz

It is clear that assessment and evaluation are priorities in current literacy initiatives, and therefore fundamental to your job as a literacy principal. Assessment and evaluation take on different guises depending on the nature of the program, from informal tools such as observations or running records, to more formal tools such as diagnostic tests or compulsory standardized tests. It is essential that you, as lead advocate for your school, understand the content implications of these methods and tests and how each type supports students' learning.

Schools represent communities of independent people who meet daily throughout the year for the betterment of all. To unite your learning community, your job as a literacy principal entails building an assessment and evaluation program that represents the heterogeneous needs of its people, while at the same time establishing a common philosophy that underpins your reading and writing curriculum. The two forces can work in unison if your program of assessment and evaluation speaks to independent student needs *and* accords with the philosophy of your overall literacy framework. In their book *A Teacher's Guide to Standardized Reading Tests*, Calkins, Montgomery, and Santman contend:

Schools need to reach out for tools to conduct our assessment sitting side by side with children.

What underlies all assessment and evaluation are three fundamental principles of good teaching — be active, be reflective, and be collaborative.

In a research report on literacy issued in 2007 by the TD Bank Financial Group, the authors summarize the effect of literacy on the workforce:

Literacy is a core ability to function in today's economy and society. For example, individuals with higher literacy scores are more likely to complete high school and pursue post-secondary education. They are more likely to succeed at college or university. After finishing their formal education, individuals with higher literacy skills are more likely to enter the labour market and to find gainful employment. (*Literacy Matters: A Call for Action*, p. 11)

Assessing and Evaluating the Whole Picture

There are as many views about assessment and evaluation as there are about acquiring literacy skills. Some educators adhere to a philosophy of reading assessment that only rigorous, long-standing diagnostic tests like the Gates–MacGinitie Reading Test can measure student progress. Although these tools carry some validity and reliability when combined with other methods, they should not be used exclusively as a reflection of a student's abilities. Instead, we promote adopting more of a mosaic of formal and informal assessment tools to evaluate student progress and to thoroughly support student learning.

Before outlining specific assessment tools to help your school build a strong reading and writing curriculum, we will define some key terms you will need to construct a curriculum that matches your school's, your teachers', and your students' needs. To clarify the two terms: *assessment* is the gathering, recording, and analysis of data about a student's progress and achievements or a program's implementation or effectiveness; *evaluation* is the application of judgment to the data gathered and its analysis, in order to place a "value" on progress, achievement, or effectiveness.

Assessment is therefore undertaken to assess the strengths and needs of a student. Essentially there are three general sources of assessment evidence in classrooms — observations of learning, products students create, and conversations about literacy development. Based on such assessment data, teachers can then make informed decisions about their overall program to determine whether or not the original objectives and approaches they set out were appropriate, and to make modifications so that the program satisfies the needs of individual students and the class as a whole. Evaluation, as Anne Davies points out in *Making Classroom Assessment Work*, comes in many forms, from descriptive feedback to more formal evaluative feedback that identifies how a student performed compared to others.

The three major types of assessment that teachers should integrate into their literacy framework include

- *Diagnostic assessment,* which can be undertaken at any time during the year to evaluate the progress of particular students and to decide whether they require some form of intervention
- *Formative assessment,* which is ongoing assessment that occurs at any time in the year to identify difficulties quickly and to provide an opportunity for immediate remedial action
- *Summative assessment,* which occurs at the end of a unit, course. or program

There is now another set of terms that parallels, in some ways, the list of diagnostic, formative, and summative assessment: assessment *for* learning (combining diagnostic and formative) and assessment *of* learning (summative). Some authors are now combining the two into a process called "assessment *as* learning."

The purpose of all of these types of assessment is to examine students' achievements in relation to some standard of excellence or in relation to some body of knowledge. It gives the teacher information about where to go next with program and instruction (for individual students and/or for the class as a whole). The ideal program of assessment and evaluation for any reading and writing curriculum outlines a process of ongoing observations of children's development with modifications and/or interventions when the need arises. Just as we need a wide repertoire of ways to help children learn to read and write, so too we should use a repertoire of assessments to evaluate all aspects of their progress so that we take into account both their strengths and their weaknesses.

Understanding Standardized Tests

Calkins, Montgomery, and Santman define a standardized test as *a test in which people are measured in a uniform way.* In their work, the authors describe *positive* types of standardized tests, such as criterion-referenced tests, and *negative* types of standardized tests, such as norm-referenced tests. According to Calkins et al., the problem with norm-referenced tests is that they are designed to produce scores that fall on a bell curve; to do this they are pre-tested by students who are supposed to represent the national average. Herein lies the problem with norm-referenced tests: they assume that all students learn at the same pace and are from a similar background. Criterion-referenced tests, on the other hand, reflect standards that have been set by such national organizations as the National Council of Teachers of English. Hence they measure what students know and can do through a variety of performances, rather than by relying solely on more of a paper-and-pencil format. What is crucial to find out about a standardized test is its construct validity; construct validity refers to how well a test measures what it purports to measure.

Provincial and state governments maintain that the goal of standardized tests lies in comparing results among schools and school boards. In theory, such an approach, as the Ontario Ministry of Education explains, *helps to identify areas that need improvement and target resources accordingly.* What "testing for a better tomorrow" means for you, as a harbinger of change, is a new dimension to your planning and monitoring of a school-wide literacy initiative that not only matches teacher and student needs but also meets curricular outcomes and expectations. Choreographing a literacy initiative in your school at times places you in a divided position because you face conflicts between meeting policy demands versus student and teacher demands.

Government tests are no doubt here to stay, but how we handle the process may determine many of the literacy outcomes for our students. School leaders have a significant role to play in setting the context for learning in school systems using standardized or norm-referenced assessments. To address the realities of teaching today, principals must recognize the underlying assumptions of standardized tests and decide how both informal and formal assessment methods can be built into a school's reading and writing curriculum.

Assessment is not cut and dried; it is not a process whereby you simply identify students who need help and commend those who are doing well. It is a complex and well-researched field of inquiry that defies standardization. Nonetheless, standardized testing is now part of teachers' and students' reality, and hence a vital aspect of your role as a model of literacy.

Here, Catherine Mulroney, a parent educational advocate, cautions us to recognize the strengths and weaknesses of the tests we inflict on our children, and to examine the resulting effects on school programs and on the culture of learning.

Testing: The Unseen Curriculum

Catherine Mulroney, The Toronto Star

The education ministry assured parents that tests were not intended to rank schools. But that's precisely what has happened. Now parents chase results like camp followers in search of the elusive perfect school, basing everything on a paper test. The benchmark of a good school is now marks and marks alone, rather than a big picture that includes report cards and regular communication with the teacher.

People aren't asking about the mood of the school, whether the children are happy or whether they demonstrate compassion and generosity and tolerance. Concern for the education all students receive in all schools is giving way to the hype surrounding published test results. For some schools, high scores are the result of teaching to the test, at the expense of regular curriculum.

Parents now seek out schools like the one my children attend (where I'm pleased to report kids seem happy despite increasing parental attention to marks), no longer satisfied with schools they'd been happy with until published results suggested they should feel otherwise.

And that's the crux of the issue. Test scores set up a smoke screen to hide larger issues in education, such as the crumbling state of many urban schools. Schools where children play amid a forest of portables. Schools constantly under the threat of losing music programs, swimming pools, librarians and other vital resources because strained budgets simply cannot be stretched any farther.

Then there's the way results are reached. Should two or three students be absent during testing week they are counted as not meeting the provincial standard, bringing down an entire grade's standings. Not accurate and not fair. And let's not even talk about the bills for all this testing. But the testing goes on. I saw the future recently when a friend from California visited with her daughter, who has written standardized tests every year since starting school. Annie is seven years old, with three tests under her belt. She'll write at least a test a year until she graduates. It's a frill students simply can't afford.

Connecting Assessment and Teaching

A fundamental part of your job as gatekeeper of literacy initiatives in your school is understanding

- What assessments and strategies to administer
- How your teachers can teach test-taking strategies
- How to respond to asssessment measures with interventions or programs
- How increased achievement scores can lead to improved reading skills

But the question remains: What will children be tested on? And, what impact will this have on their education? We are not suggesting devoting valuable teaching time to "teaching to the test," but, instead, facilitating a meta-awareness of tests, test-taking strategies, and how assessment works within a balanced literacy framework.

To create an effective assessment and evaluation program in your school you have to encourage teachers to combine a variety of informal assessments with such diagnostic tools as the Gates–MacGinitie Reading Test or the Yopp Singer

See Authentic Reading Assessment by Steven Reid on page 131.

Phonemic Segmentation Test, as well as compulsory tests mandated by provincial or state governments. Indeed, to tackle the challenge of more formal assessments, such as annual standardized tests, it is necessary to develop a reading curriculum that works from the inside out.

When we speak of creating an assessment program from the inside out, we are referring to the assessment and evaluation that grows out of students' needs. Teachers and their principals must have high expectations for each child's success, and support development and learning with appropriate and supportive attention that embraces each child's interests and needs. The ideal school culture is one that does not highlight errors and mistakes, but instead focuses on what children can do, through observation and assessment, and recognizes the possibilities that lie ahead for each child. Teachers need to see mistakes as part of the learning process, and to use the knowledge that they have gleaned from the children's attempts in order to offer support and instruction in literacy techniques.

Anne Davies, in *Making Classroom Assessment Work,* uses the metaphor of assessment as inukshuks, or markers made of stone that guide travelers to their destination. In planning a literacy initiative in your school, it may be useful to regard assessment and evaluation as navigating a course for each student. What this implies is simultaneously — and, we might add paradoxically — individualizing and standardizing. In short, ask your teachers to find the right tools to assess students' reading and writing abilities, evaluate or diagnose their individual progress, and juxtapose this against the norm (i.e., compare to results among other schools and school boards).

There is a large repository of research and writing on assessment and evaluation that comes to bear on this philosophy for assessing young readers and writers. Here, Anne Davies indicates the three salient findings about assessment that we now know due to work in the field by such researchers as Purkey and Novak; Schon; Black and Wiliam; Hurry; and Davies herself.

- When students take ownership of their own assessment, they are required to think about their learning and articulate their understandings, which correspondingly helps them learn
- When students are involved in their own assessment, mistakes become feedback and they get to make choices about their progress
- When the amount of descriptive feedback is increased and the amount of evaluative feedback is decreased, student learning increases significantly

In the end, what is clear from research, theory, and practice is that it is important to assess *all* areas of children's development to improve literacy standards in your school. To do this, you need to gather information from a variety of sources, including consulting the writings of others, as well as communicating with and consulting teachers, students, and parents to crystallize what exactly you need to do to create successful literacy-based change.

Deciding What to Assess

Before deciding on a particular mode or tool for assessment, it is useful to consider the breadth of what needs to be assessed in literacy. The chart on page 122 is derived from a report researched and written by the Center for the Improvement of Early Reading Achievement (CIERA) and is offered as an example of what needs to be assessed in the early stages of reading development. It includes five literacy categories and their constituent knowledge, skills, and attitudes. Obviously, this list is merely representative of the myriad items that need to be considered at each stage of literacy development, but it at least provides a start for your school's considerations of what needs to be assessed.

Some Ways of Assessing

See Data-Driven Writing Programs by Mary Reid on page 137.

As has been discussed already, in choosing suitable modes and tools for assessment, the goal is to create assessment-friendly classrooms where the staff understand the foundations of the reading and writing processes and incorporate techniques and strategies that enable each child to achieve success. It is with this in mind that we present a series of possible modes and tools of assessment from which you and your staff can create an assessment and evaluation program. Given the plethora of skills, backgrounds, and types of learners in classrooms, it is essential to have versatility and breadth in your assessment and evaluation program. We present these modes and tools not as a prescription for assessment, but instead as a series of suggested assessment activities you can use to structure your school's reading and writing curriculum.

In the pages that follow, we describe key modes and tools of assessment that have proven successful in indicating a child's literacy progress. We list the items from more informal measures to formal measures of reading and writing development, in order to reinforce our belief in balancing formalized approaches with daily, weekly, and monthly informal approaches to assess literacy development.

Observation

When we observe children during literacy events, we bring to the process our knowledge of the theory of language learning and the practical aspects of teaching children to read and write. There are two types of observation: close observation and distance observation.

When possible, teachers should tape children's discussions and presentations. Viewing the tapes away from the hustle and bustle of the classroom provides them with information relating to children's level of and type of participation in groups, the level of discussions in which children engage, and individual strengths and weaknesses.

Close observation involves observing a child for a period of five minutes while she or he reads or writes. During close observation, the teacher might note such features of the reading process as the reading strategies a child uses; aspects of the text that appear to be challenging; and what the child does when she or he encounters difficulty. Distance observation involves watching such reading behaviors as how a child selects a book, reads independently, or moves around during the activity. To observe children to a sufficient degree, teachers need to make observations of one or two children each day, or devote one day a week to observation.

When observing students, your staff should bear in mind the following six fundamental stages in setting a literacy program:

- Know the strategies of proficient reading and writing
- Observe and record students' interests and attitudes
- Choose appropriate procedures
- Use the procedures effectively and efficiently
- Develop appropriate strategy lessons
- Determine reporting procedures

Literacy Category	Knowledge, Skills, and Attitudes
Concepts about Print	• Has concept of letter or word • Understands directionality • Identifies parts of a book • Labels pictures • Understands letter and word order • Has a sense of story • Understands punctuation marks • Understands that print conveys meaning • Understands upper- and lower-case letters • Recognizes word boundaries
Attitude	• Has a good attitude toward literacy activities • Enjoys reading • Exhibits good reading behaviors • Exhibits good writing behaviors
Reading Comprehension	• Knows the topic of a book • Wants to become more fluent • Identifies own name • Is developing some accuracy • Has reading flexibility • Chooses appropriate texts • Uses book language • Monitors own reading strategies • Uses self-correction methods • Uses pictures and story line for predicting context and words • Uses print for predicting meaning of the text • Comments on literary aspects of the text • Connects personal experiences with text • Distinguishes fantasy from realistic texts • Draws conclusions • Identifies cause–effect relationships • Makes inferences • Provides supporting details • Retells • Knows the sequence of story events • Summarizes main ideas
Motivation	• Refers books to others • Is motivated to read • Uses family support and prior experience to read • Has reading preferences • Responds to literature • Reads for own purposes • Spends time reading
Metacognition	• Has familiarity with types of texts • Is able to monitor reading • Is aware of personal progress • Plans how to read • Exhibits reading-related behaviors • Self-assesses in non-language arts domains too • Self reviews • Shares with others • Executes strategies for how to read • Incorporates teacher feedback • Has writing-related behaviors

Observation Guides and Checklists

It is essential to bear in mind that observation guides and checklists are precisely that — indicators of a child's progress. Once again, the key to any effective literacy initiative lies in combining several assessment tools simultaneously, so that no one guide can be viewed as absolute.

Checklists and guides are most valuable when they are repeated several times throughout the year. In this way, trends and progress that occur over the year can be noted. For example, in the case of reading, they can help show how a child is developing as a reader — level of fluency, use of strategies, and awareness of cueing systems. As Anne Davies notes, observations arising from checklists can be shared with children too, to encourage them to take responsibility for their learning by focusing on areas that require change.

Your teachers may wish to try a published tool such as Marie Clay's Observation Survey for assessing reading development. This informal reading assessment tool assesses concepts about print by applying a criterion-referenced approach to reading development and is targeted for emergent literacy learners. The aim of Clay's Observation Survey is to help students develop independent reading strategies such as cross-checking, self-monitoring, and searching for meaning. It measures letter identification, concepts about print, sight word reading, and hearing and recording sounds in oral reading and writing vocabulary.

Anecdotal Records

Anecdotal records are those that teachers make on an informal basis as they observe children in their day-to-day learning. Given the nature of these observations, many teachers choose to make notes on index cards or a small notepad. Individual cards or sheets from the notepad can then be stored in open files. A teacher may choose to observe children by groups or on an individual basis.

Students often provide a lot of useful information in inventories, and anecdotal recording is one way of keeping track of this information. Inventories, where children complete a list of their achievements, favorite activities, or interests, can be extremely helpful when planning topics to explore in class. Additionally, inventories can tell a teacher about children's feelings related to aspects of their learning and information that may not be visible in class.

Ideally, children can complete an inventory like a reading-attitudes inventory either in writing or orally when they begin school in September, and these can then be updated throughout the year. In this way a teacher can learn about negative or indifferent attitudes early and try to discover the reasons for these through other methods, such as those described below.

Reading Interviews

What students believe about reading and reading instruction affects their decisions about strategies to use during reading. A reading interview is a series of open-ended questions designed to tell you

- The strategies used by proficient and inefficient readers
- How students cope with difficult material
- What qualities typify "good" readers, according to students
- What reading strategies students would recommend to others
- Students' personal strengths and weaknesses

Reading interviews should be conducted in an informal setting relatively free from interruption. Notations of students' responses can be written or taped. A teacher may wish to conduct reading interviews several times during the year to determine if attitudes have changed and if there has been development in students' knowledge about the process of proficient reading.

In examining students' responses, a teacher can speculate on the ways in which their reading proficiency has been influenced by previous reading instruction. The kinds of information the interview reveals, along with teacher observations, can be used to design appropriate reading experiences for each student. As well, the results can be discussed with students to determine the different kinds of strategies they use as readers.

Retelling

Employing retelling of a text as a form of assessment and evaluation promotes a meta-awareness of text content, design, and structure. It also facilitates a greater awareness of the variety of texts made available to students over the course of their learning. According to Hazel Brown and Brian Cambourne in *Read and Retell*:

> The retelling procedure, as we define it, coerces learners to bring to their conscious awareness of many features of text structure on which they would not typically focus, or upon which they would not typically reflect.

By sharing retellings with peers, students make explicit what would previously have been primarily implicit and have the opportunity to apply their previous knowledge and experience to new types of texts.

In their research, Brown and Cambourne found that, if teachers sample students' retellings over time and use them in conjunction with other assessment tools, they can make evaluative statements about

- Reading ability
- Knowledge of various genres
- Control of many aspects of written language
- Control of many aspects of the writing process

Retelling provides a rich and detailed picture of a student's language development over time.

Running Records

A running record, like miscue analysis, presents a record of a child's reading behavior on a specific text. It was developed by Dr. Marie Clay in New Zealand. In this procedure, a teacher sits beside a child while the child reads a text, so that both the teacher and the child are looking at the same text. The child reads a text that she or he has read before, although on occasion a new text might be read once or twice as a final assessment of progress.

The text should be one that presents some challenges so that the teacher can observe the problem-solving strategies the child is using. However, it should not be so difficult that the child cannot continue to read. Otherwise, the child cannot put into use the strategies that she or he possesses, resorting to guessing or to sounding words out at the expense of understanding the meaning.

In one district, principals provided support for teachers by providing access to in-service on running records, learning resources for students such as "leveled" books, and specialist reading teachers. The principals themselves increased their knowledge of reading instruction by participating in a session in which they observed a teacher modeling the administration of a running record and then conducted a few running records themselves. They also met in peer groups to discuss progress in their schools, devise strategies for supporting their teachers, and respond to input on school change from university staff.

Based on Marie Clay's research, a teacher adopts a coding system that determines a student's reading strategies and use of cueing systems by regularly charting reading development on a running record. As a student is reading, the teacher observes closely, coding the child's reading attempts on a form using symbols Marie Clay developed as a modified reading record. In this way, a teacher acts as an observer rather than as an instructor, recording all of the information the child reads. If a child cannot continue because of a difficult word, the teacher can tell the child the word so that the reader can move forward and maintain fluency.

Portfolio Conferences

Portfolio conferences about reading are an invaluable source of information about children's reading experiences. In this type of assessment, children bring several journal entries to a conference to discuss their growth as readers with their teachers. Informal discussion questions may relate to the number of books read, the number of books begun but not finished, and the reasons for this. Based on the results of such a conference, a teacher may conduct reading inventories and/or set new goals with students (e.g., setting a number of pages or books to be read; reading books from another genre, etc.).

Portfolio conferences can take place between a teacher and a child, between peers, or between a parent and a child. Of these configurations, teacher–child conferences are essential, peer conferences are desirable (depending on the age of the children), and child–parent conferences are recommended. The teacher's conferences with children are essential for the development of self-assessment skills. Only after a teacher conference occurs with each child should the children participate in other types of conferences. Ongoing child–teacher conferences may culminate in child-led parent–child conferences at the end of the year.

Checklist of Comprehension Strategies

A checklist of comprehension strategies enables a teacher to observe to what degree a student is employing the strategies of a proficient or inefficient reader. Proficient reading strategies are identified and put on a continuum, which the teacher can then use as a checklist to record his or her observations of a student's reading behavior and progress. A continuum from 1 (least proficient) to 5 (greatest proficiency) works best.

On the basis of observations of a student's reading, the teacher places a check mark on the continuum at the place that most closely represents the student's use of each comprehension strategy. One checklist is required for each student. A student whose proficiency falls within the 1 to 2 range on an item on the checklist likely requires reading strategy lessons.

Literature Circles for Self-Evaluation

A literature circle typically comprises three to five children who are reading the same book and who come together in small heterogeneous groups to discuss, react, and share responses. The purpose of the circle is to promote reading and responses to literature through discussions and to provide opportunities for children to work in child-directed small groups.

Taping a session can help the teacher to observe the dynamics of the group and the literacy behavior of its members. As well, group members can view the tape after completing discussions on the book in order to reflect on their contributions and the process. As a follow-up to that, members should be encouraged to self-reflect using their journals.

At the beginning, the teacher often selects the book and assigns children to groups. As time progresses, children should be encouraged to choose from among three or four books, giving them some control over their own learning, and to form their own groups. The teacher generally monitors the groups and may join a group to add to the discussion. Literature circles usually meet three times per week for a period of 15 to 30 minutes, and can last from one day to six weeks, depending on the length of a book. Journals can be used as both a follow-up to literature circle discussions and as preparation for future discussions.

Personal Response

Personal response is an account of the transaction that occurs between the reader and the text as meaning evolves. Personal response is an essential first step in reading. Personal response reflects what a story, poem, or play says to the reader and what the reader says to the story. Because of readers' diverse backgrounds and attitudes, variations in reactions to a text are inevitable and legitimate. This form of assessment accounts for and indeed legitimizes subjective interpretations of texts.

The assessment of personal response can occur as students engage in a variety of activities, such as class or group discussions, or drama, art, or music activities related to books. In the case of assessing personal response, it is helpful to find out where children are as readers as early in the school year as possible. This process would include an investigation of students'

Instruments to help in this assessment might include general interest inventories, reading interest inventories, teacher–student conferences, personal reading-record cards, personal response journal entries, and observations, both formal and informal.

- General interests
- Perceptions of literature
- Favorite books or genres
- Readiness with which they become involved in what they read
- Habitual approach to a type of book, particularly fiction
- Interpretations and perceptions of what they read

As a result of this type of assessment, teachers can direct students to further reading materials that will match their interests and ability to read and comprehend with independence. As well, teachers can help students to make stronger connections between themes and ideas in literature.

Reading Logs

By encouraging students to keep logs in which they record their reading progress in general, teachers can encourage children to reflect upon themselves as readers. Logs generally indicate the extent of growth of independence in reading, as students gain confidence and skills in their ability to interact with printed materials.

To implement reading logs, teachers need to provide folders for students to keep their records. Students then bring their folder to individual reading conferences. The logs can help teachers and students to discover

- Reading interests
- Quantity of material being read
- Breadth of reading

Depending on the results, teachers may wish to redirect students to different types of reading material in order to encourage wider reading or, if students are reading very little, may wish to administer a reading inventory to help explain why this is so.

Cloze Procedures

Cloze procedures involve oral or written deletions of parts of words, whole words, or phrases in a passage of text. "Clozing," or restoring these gaps, requires children to scan the text, recognize and process contextual cues, and then choose the most appropriate word or phrase. In this way, the reader learns to use context to help figure out unfamiliar words in an active and constructive language process.

Cloze activities are suitable for use at all grade levels and can help to build a number of skills exhibited by strong, fluent readers, including

- Focusing on contextual cueing systems
- Ability to anticipate the text to make the most sense
- Interaction with text, such as searching, scanning, and thinking, that can result in making meaning with print
- A repertoire of thinking strategies
- Confidence in ability to predict in order to recognize words
- General reading ability, comprehension, and vocabulary awareness

An example of a cloze activity is the following homophone cloze:

I was ___ tired __ read the last ___ pages.

Answer: I was too tired to read the last two pages.

Deletions can target particular types of words, as in the example above, or can be made arbitrarily. Cloze procedures can also target parts of words you would like to assess and in which your students need practice. On the whole, cloze procedures are a useful way of assessing children's reading ability, comprehension, and vocabulary.

Profiles of Writing Behavior

Profiles can be created at the beginning of the year to get a general picture of each child's writing behaviors and strategies. They can then be used at intervals throughout the year to monitor those students whose strategies do not seem to be productive. Profiles might be used as a basis for a sustained observation of one student, or to observe a number of students at five-minute intervals throughout a writing session to see the activities students are engaged in.

A profile of writing behavior may help answer such questions as

- Does the student understand what should be done at each stage of the writing process?
- Does the student use avoidance strategies, such as pencil-sharpening or collecting materials, to delay getting started on the task?
- Is the student having regular conferences with peers and with the teacher?
- What does the student want to discuss during conferences?
- Does the student sustain writing for long periods?
- Is the student a confident writer or is constant reassurance necessary?
- Does the student use print sources to get information?

Exemplars as Benchmarks

In response to more structured language curriculum, provincial and state governments have produced documents which furnish examples of high and low achievement in reading and writing in Grades 1 to 8. Exemplars are intended to serve as models for boards, schools, and teachers in setting reading and writing tasks.

As the Ontario Ministry of Education explains, using exemplars over the course of a literacy initiative can help you and your staff to identify students' reading and writing levels in the following ways:

- Show characteristics of student work at each level of achievement for each grade
- Promote greater consistency in the assessment of student work from grade to grade and across provinces and states
- Provide an approach to improving student learning by showing children's written work completed at their level
- Offer clear criteria by which to assess students' written work
- Illustrate the connections between what students are expected to learn and how their work can be assessed on the basis of levels of achievement

You are by no means obligated to use a government's version of exemplars, although they do furnish a blueprint for your own development of a set of rubrics. You and your staff can cull examples of student work that match different levels of achievement and collectively create your own rubrics. For example, you and your staff may wish to collect samples of writing assignments or journal entries that show the range of writing in a given grade and bring these samples to a staff meeting to discuss and come to a consensus as to why you think certain samples belong in a respective level. Schools can thereby create their own set of exemplars that they can use as benchmarks throughout the school year.

Informal and Formal Tests

Tests, both informal and formal, are helpful when they assess learning that is measurable and when they reflect the content of the program. However, in reading and writing, many components cannot be isolated. For this reason, interpretation of tests must be handled carefully. If information gleaned from a test does not reflect a teacher's ongoing assessment data, the testing device may need to be altered. A less likely scenario involves the teacher adjusting his or her ongoing assessment.

If both the test and the instruction are sound, it is important to keep in mind that there are a number of reasons why a child may not perform well on an isolated test, ranging from a bad night's rest to a problem at home. Test results should be viewed by you, your staff, and the students as a way to check the effectiveness of the program. In this way, children will feel less anxious and not be concerned that a poor test result will influence their learning for the rest of the year.

In some locations, as discussed earlier in the chapter, class-wide testing is becoming more common. Much has been made in some areas of lower-than-expected results, and a call for action has resulted. What educators need to keep in mind, just as in individual cases, is that a variety of factors may influence reading and writing results. One evident example is a class where the majority of the class speak English as a second language. Such a factor must be taken into account when discussing lower than expected results. It is also important to consider the fact that in such situations, one test for all may not be the most effective measure.

Reflecting on Assessment

- How might your school begin to examine its policies and articulate a plan for assessing the progress of children in various grades and divisions?
- In what ways could your staff most effectively share the assessment strategies, checklists, guides, etc. that they have collected and find helpful for assessing various literacy concepts, skills, and attitudes?
- How can teachers use ideas such as concrete demonstrations of children's growth (e.g., writing folders) for preparing for teacher–parent conferences?
- How can teachers use the questions that arise during teacher–parent conferences as a starting point for further communications, such as personal letters, newsletters, copies of articles, or student self-assessment reports?

- How can your school enlist the help of parents in the whole process of assessment?
- How might your school use occasional reading and writing assessment tools across the whole school in a way that is most beneficial to all?
- How can you and your staff ensure that in administering such tests as standardized tests that the results are seen as information rather than as grades, and that comparisons among individual teachers and individual students are not made?
- How can the results of schoolwide assessments be used as the basis for overall discussions about students' competencies and potential, as well as to establish benchmarks for growth?

Concluding Thoughts

For many educators, the tasks of planning, monitoring, and then assessing and evaluating children's literacy development are complex and increasingly fragmented tasks. By complex, we are referring in particular to the challenge of assessing children's literacy skills, evaluating their progress, adapting programs to meet their needs, and ideally preserving an even progression of their literacy development.

There are four main participants who must take centre stage in assessing and evaluating literacy skills: you, the principal, as the lead advocate for a balanced assessment program; your teachers as the primary recorders of students' behavior and work; your students as self-assessors and record keepers; and your students' parents as valuable sources of information, insights, and observations about their children, as well as partners in the campaign to help children become literate.

As we have tried to highlight throughout the chapter, creating a mosaic of assessment and evaluation tools offers greater precision and ultimately more support for students. A strong assessment program relies on merging a hybrid of assessment tools that speak to the multiple needs of students. To conciliate the formal with the informal, the goal should be to acquire both formal and informal data from student learning to evaluate students' attitudes toward literacy and language development and to draw conclusions about students' overall development of literacy skills.

What we hoped to model in this chapter are assessment and evaluation procedures that are student-centred, that keep language and thought intact, and that have comprehension at their centre. In addition, we have deliberately presented an overall assessment program that takes into account a continuum of assessment tools, from informal ones to formalized ones. To return to our main message, we not only need to understand the assumptions, the content, the design, and the intentions of assessment tools, but also to coach children on every aspect of an assessment program.

Since we are working in a pedagogy that combines multiple and at times contrary perspectives on assessment, it is your job as a literacy principal to unify them so that all students have an opportunity to improve their literacy standards.

Some Suggestions for Fair Testing Practice
Regie Routman

Work to ensure that your school and district testing practices are developmentally appropriate and fair to children. This is no easy matter. With so much pressure for high test scores, inappropriate practices are rampant. Get together with your colleagues.

Take a hard look at how you prepare students for high-stakes testing. While it's absolutely necessary to prepare your students for tests, is your focus and time spent reasonable? Do students understand why and what they are being prepared for?

Decide how you can adjust your daily teaching so that assessment is part of instruction and not separate from it. The traditional school structure does not build in time for assessment or stress the importance of ongoing assessment. As we did, you may want to start a study group. (Many of us met for months through our language arts support group. Without those conversations, student-led conferences would never have become a reality.)

(*from* Conversations: Strategies for Teaching, Learning and Evaluation, *2000)*

Authentic Reading Assessment

Steven Reid

Steven Reid is Superintendent of Instruction with the Bluewater District School Board. Previously, he was the Central Coordinating Principal of Elementary Curriculum with the Toronto District School Board, and served a secondment as an Education Officer with the Ministry of Education.

When I contributed to the first edition of *The Literacy Principal*, I was fairly new to the principal's role in a school involved in a large-scale literacy project. Since that time, I have had the wonderful opportunity to work with the Ministry of Education as an Education Officer, focusing on leadership development in the area of assessment literacy. Another role — central principal of elementary instruction — enabled me to consider the big picture by asking the question, "How can we ensure consistency and effectiveness of instructional practice in hundreds of schools across the district?" Currently, I am embracing my role as superintendent of instruction. Similarly, the focus of this role involves supporting professional learning environments to develop lateral and vertical capacity-building and alignment to ensure high levels of student success.

Over the past year, I have kept one particular quote as part of my e-mail signature, for this quote promotes many wonderful discussions and debates with both principals and teachers. The lead up to this quote is as follows:

> The skillful use of classroom data allows us to identify strengths and weaknesses in student learning, monitor student progress towards specific goals, make adjustment in instruction, measure the degree to which students meet standards, and distinguish between effective and ineffective instructional practice. (Fox, 2001)

I used this portion of the quote as I worked with many leadership teams and principal groups, and there is never much debate. The overall concept of using assessment data to support student learning and focus effective instructional practices is a viewed as a worthy goal. As a principal, it is invaluable to observe this quote manifested as reality … at times, it's like magic. It is a learning opportunity to spend time in a classroom where the teacher is a master at regularly conferencing with students to work through a running record, review a reading response journal, or listen to a retelling of a text. At a recent Principal Qualification Program course, I asked future administrative leaders to consider the following:

- How will you ensure that all students learn to read and write at high levels?
- How will you support capacity building of effective instructional strategies to support high levels of reading?
- How will you support learning environments that allow teachers to analyze student work, review school-wide data, and promote the sharing of effective practices?
- How will you ensure that assessment for learning is embedded in the culture of the school?

The answers to these questions provide the excitement of the principal's role. I suggested, that if the principals-to-be did not find excitement in promoting professional learning, focusing on student achievement results, and building a strong culture of inquiry in their schools, then this was not the role for them. Of course this was said with a grin; however, in every joke there is a kernel of truth.

On a district level, we know that our principals are key to the ultimate success of any school. There is a large body of research that clearly demonstrates the strong influence that the principal has on student achievement (Waters, Marzano and McNulty, 2003).

Let's get to the heart of the matter, the next sentence in the quote that causes educators to consider their practice in the classroom and, ultimately, the consistency of assessment practices in the school and district. Fox amplifies the importance of data with the statement,

> Without data, instruction becomes a series of well-intentioned, but "random acts of teaching."

As a leader, this is your reason for developing an assessment framework within your school, for it is without a doubt true that teachers and principals do not have time for instructional randomness. Each minute of the school day must be focused on the specific strengths and needs of the student. Time is of the essence — we know that a student requires the skills of reading and writing by the end of his/her primary years; otherwise, the child will struggle throughout school. I will extend Fox's statement for the principal:

> Without data, principalship becomes a series of well-intentioned, but "random acts of leadership."

We can certainly replace the word "principal" with "superintendent" or "director." With this in mind, I will discuss the assessment framework and the structures surrounding assessment of reading within a school and district that promote student achievement and professional learning.

Assessment Framework

As a principal, I find a never-ending part of the role is working through the Review/Develop/ Implement cycle. Whether you are new to the school or started at the school as a teacher, reviewing or "surveying the land" is critical. In considering reading, you need to continually gather information about the following:

- What highly effective instructional strategies are being used in the classrooms
- What professional learning opportunities to further explore reading instruction and assessment exist for teachers
- How students are guided to deeper understandings and connections with the materials they read
- What types of reading assessments are commonly used in classrooms
- How learning is monitored and addressed

An essential step in delving deeply into these questions involves the development of an Assessment Framework; unless we know where students are on the learning continuum, there is no sense of urgency to answer these questions in any depth. If we believe our students are doing as well as they can, why would we spend the time to further investigate reading instruction or cross-curricular reading opportunities?

From your review of the school, you will know what types of reading assessments are being used (e.g., running records, observation surveys, reading interest and attitude surveys, response to texts). At the classroom level, teachers will use many forms of assessments to build a strong picture of each student's strengths and needs. At the school level, an assessment framework is developed to gather certain reading assessment results throughout the year to monitor overall progress to school-based goals.

A Sample of a Literacy Assessment Framework	
Term 1 September to October	Common Reading Assessment(s) *Examples* • Clay's Observation Survey • Running Records • PM Benchmark • Developmental Reading Assessment • CASI
Term 2 January to February	
Term 3 May to June	Common Writing Assessment(s) *Examples* • Ontario Writing Assessment • First Steps

Professional learning communities, school leadership teams, school improvement teams, and grade/division groupings use the results gathered through the assessment framework to identify what progress is occurring and what needs to change. We cannot wait until the end of the year to determine what effect our efforts are having on student learning. Once again, time is of the essence. The power that the assessment framework can have on a learning organization is magnified by the inclusion of common assessments, developing high standards for student achievement, and setting targets based on trend data.

Common Assessments

When common assessments are chosen at the school or district level, many benefits are provided to staff:

• Common language: assessment, criteria, expectations, levels of achievement
• Tracking achievement: individual, group, and cohort achievement can be tracked during the year and throughout grades offered at the school
• Comparison points: common assessments can be compared to various data points, such as report cards, district-wide assessments, provincial or state assessments, reading vs. writing
• Teacher moderation: bringing teachers together to score common assessments and determine next steps

As common assessments are introduced into the school, professional development is essential. At first, the mechanics of the assessment will often surface as the level of concern; i.e., how does the teacher implement this assessment in the classroom (individual, group, whole-class) and how is the assessment scored? As the mechanics of the assessment implementation are reviewed, the most important issue comes to the forefront: How will this assessment help my instruction? As a principal, you must ensure that this question is answered and consistently investigated at deeper levels. For example, many primary reading assessments rely on a running record. At the initial stages of implementation, the conversation often revolves around the reading "level" assigned to the student. Although the level tells the teacher something about the student's reading ability, this in itself is not enough to program effectively for the child. It is important to then consider the types of miscues that the student made while achieving that level in reading; i.e., should future programming for the student involve further understanding of graphic, meaning, and/or structure of the text. As you continue to focus assessment on digging deeper to further understand the student, you foster a culture of learning for all.

Digging Deeper with Assessment

Our board-wide literacy assessment framework includes CASI and the Ontario Writing Assessment at the junior and intermediate levels. Here is an example of some of the data investigated and questions asked during various professional learning opportunities for literacy teachers and principals.

COHORT DATA DURING THE YEAR

School teams review their cohort data:

- What gains were made to the board-wide standard in second and third term
- Students who did not make standard, what progress did they make
- What strategies or initiatives were in place to support students; were they successful
- Students who did not make standard; how will we support them in the new year

IDENTIFYING NEXT STEPS

Turning the data gathered from a common reading assessment into information about the learning needs of students is vital. This information is then used to guide instructional planning for individual students, groups of students, and the whole class. Identifying next steps in reading will also involve considering next steps in writing:

Connecting writing activities to the reading process where possible helps strengthen overall literacy development. When writing and reading are combined, children have the opportunity to put into practice their awareness of how print works (Booth & Rowsell, 2002).

To support the connection between reading and writing, teams review writing common assessment results (Ontario Writing Assessment) asking similar questions to map out next steps.

School term results on a common reading assessment (CASI):

- What percentage of students made standard?
- Are there differences between female and male results?
- What categories are strengths and needs for the cohort (knowledge and understanding, thinking, communication, application)?
- Are there results for particular students that are surprising?
- What students require additional supports to make standard?
- What accommodations and/or modifications supported students reading?
- How will these results inform our professional learning communities and school program plan?

Student Names	CASI Questions								Overall	Overall K & U	Overall Thinking	Overall Comm.	Overall Applic.	EQAO			m/f
	#1	#2	#3	#4	#5	#6	#7	#8						R	W	M	
Emily	3	3	4	3	4	4	4	3	3.8	4.2	4.2	4.5	4.5	3	3	3	F
Brittany	2	2	3	1	2	2	3	2	2.5	2.5	2.8	3.5	3.5	3	3	3	F
Larrissa	3	3	4	4	3	3	4	3	3.8	4.2	3.8	4.5	4.5	3	3	3	F
Robbie	2	1	3	2	2	2	2	2	2.5	2.8	2.5	3.5	2.5	2	3	2	M
Jamie	2	1	4	2	3	3	2	2	2.8	3.2	2.8	4.5	2.5	2	2	3	M
Jesse	2	3	3	3	3	2	3	3	3.2	3.5	3.5	3.5	3.5	3	3	3	M
Michelle	4	3	4	4	4	3	3	3	3.8	4.8	3.8	4.5	3.5	3	3	3	F
Emily	3	1	3	2	2	1	2	2	2.5	3.2	2.2	3.5	2.5	3	2	2	F
									3.1	3.3	3.2	3.8	3.1	Overall Mean			
									3.4	3.6	3.4	4	3.4	Female Overall Mean			
									2.8	3	2.9	3.4	2.8	Male Overall Mean			

Individual teachers, grade teams, leadership teams, school improvement teams develop plans for next steps based on identified strengths and needs, such as

- Students having difficulty connecting reading passages with personal experiences

Possible Strategies to support further learning:

- Questioning: Question, Answer, Relationships (QAR)
- Literary Letters
- Literature Circles

Connecting to the Big Picture

As a leader in education, you are committed to the success of all students, including students beyond your own school. In order to promote high levels of achievement across the system, we must move beyond pockets of success. Success must be shared to promote consistency of effective practice and knowledge building. The following big-picture items can be incorporated in one school, but benefits cumulate when implemented district-wide.

MINIMUM STANDARDS / HIGH EXPECTATIONS

- Minimum standards are set for common assessment at each grade level.

  e.g., On The Mark reading assessment
Junior Kindergarten	Level A
Senior Kindergarten	Level C
Grade 1	Level J
Grade 2	Level N
Grade 3	Level R

- This provides teachers with a picture of the reading levels students should minimally achieve at each grade level to promote success at the next grade.
- School improvement teams can set targets for the number of students that will reach the minimal standard by first and second term, and by the end of the year.
- In time, schools should observe patterns of higher percentages of students reaching the standard each year.
- At a district level, targets should exemplify a belief that "all students can achieve at high levels," thus reinforcing high expectations for all students.

SCHOOL PROGRAM PLANS

- School program plans need to be viewed as a work in progress, not a final product.
- Data is required to be a central part of focusing on
  – Needs and priorities
  – Strategies to support learning and intervention
  – Goal setting
  – Personnel required to support the strategies
  – Timelines and budget
  – Evidence of success
- Schools visit with superintendents, principals, and leadership teams focus on progress toward the goals and targets highlighted in the school program plan.

PROFESSIONAL LEARNING COMMUNITIES

- Data, student achievement, and learning are central to professional learning communities.
- Professional learning communities are necessary at all levels of a district (teachers, curriculum leaders, principals, and central staff).
- Budget is set aside to allow for professional learning communities during the school day.

- Learning is shared with others to contribute to knowledge building within a school and district.

Conclusion

As a principal, you'll want to ensure that discussions about reading with your staff move beyond the collegial. You will consistently bring the talk to discussions concerning specific actions and outcomes as they pertain directly to student achievement in reading. In doing so, you support staff in reflecting on current practice and then mapping out next steps. As a leader, you must ask yourself the questions: In what ways can we gather information over time to determine our impact on the reading abilities of students? Are we moving forward as a school? Are we discussing real-time data, discussing achievement of students "in the now"?

Your goal is to observe improved student achievement in literacy, closing the gap. This is the exciting part of the role as a literacy principal — monitoring and supporting the learning around us and continually striving toward improved student success.

Data-Driven Writing Programs
Mary Reid

Mary Reid is an elementary principal in Walkerton, Ontario. Previously, she served as an Education Officer with the Education Quality and Accountability Office, and as a Literacy Instructional Leader with the Toronto District School Board.

Learning how to become an effective writer is a highly complex process. Writing involves using a wide range of skills and tasks to construct meaningful messages for various audiences and purposes…. As a teacher, you require an understanding of each student's strengths and gaps in writing skills in order to plan and implement a targeted writing program. When you are able to provide explicit instructional strategies based on this assessment, you help students develop the skills necessary to become effective writers for a variety of audiences and purposes.

Reid & Reid, *Ontario Writing Assessment*, 2007

As a first-year principal of twinned schools, I felt eager and nervous about the tremendous responsibility I had for approximately 450 students. My entry plan included being highly visible in the school, fostering a warm and inviting environment, and making well-informed decisions dictated by the data.

What the Data Was Telling Us

Our preliminary provincial results were hot off the press. I downloaded them as soon as they were made available. I had a group of teachers eagerly waiting at the printer for our school's report — complete with graphs and data for the current year and the previous four years. We were happy and not surprised to see that our Grade 3 students continued to maintain high scores. Our lowest area was writing, yet we still surpassed the board and provincial results.

In the Grade 6 scores, there appeared to be a downward trend in writing. Over the last three years, our writing scores had been decreasing, whereas the province writing levels had been steadily increasing. A mere 36% of our Grade 6 students reached the provincial standard in writing. The provincial data didn't paint a full picture; we needed to gather more evidence. So we began to look closely at daily writing samples across the school. We also administered a common writing assessment (Ontario Writing Assessment) from SK to Grade 8. The various assessment results were consistent; it was clear that our students' had gaps in their writing skills. Our journey of inquiry began to unfold.

Based on the writing assessment data, it was determined that our school would focus on targeting our teaching to improve students' writing skills. The first step in our journey was to understand the newly arrived provincial Language Curriculum. Teachers required time and direction in comprehending the revised achievement categories and the grade-by-grade curriculum expectations.

We also spent a great deal of time building a consistent understanding of the major text forms. *Literacy for Learning: The Report of the Expert Panel on Literacy in Grades 4 to 6 in Ontario* states:

> Students need to be aware of many different text forms if they are to compose
> with increasing independence for a variety of purposes across subject areas
> (Ontario Ministry of Education, 2006: 83).

We had various interpretations of text forms, and in some cases grades did not expose students to specific forms of writing. We were able to iron out our knowledge and understanding of the text forms with support materials from the Ministry of Education. Based on this, we devised a school-wide writing plan that laid out the scope and sequence of teaching the forms of writing. We collectively agreed that students require exposure to all text forms throughout the year, but some grades might delve deeper in certain forms than others.

Principal Visibility

Being visible in the classroom was one of my top priorities as a principal. Spending time in classrooms and interacting with children became the highlight of my school day. I truly appreciated and acknowledged the evidence of learning in each room. Early in the fall, while I was visiting a Grades 1/2 class, I had a student tell me, "You don't look like a principal, you look like a teacher." I asked her why she thought that. She replied, "Because you're always asking us questions about our reading and writing, just like our teacher — and plus you don't wear a fancy tie." I responded to her and said "I'm really a teacher; I'm just called a principal because someone needs to sign all the papers." She looked at me with surprised eyes, "You're really a teacher! I just knew it!" Having this candid conversation made me realize that high visibility in the classroom helps to establish relationships with students in a positive way.

As I spent more time walking through classrooms, I quickly learned how this provided me with real-time data about students' writing skills. My visibility in the classrooms enabled me to observe first-hand what students were writing about. I valued how the Kindergarten students wrote their wonderful messages, and "translated" their pictures and scribbles with great enthusiasm. To witness early/emergent writers develop over time was priceless. With targeted teaching and continual monitoring, the Kindergarten youngsters made significant progress. Toward mid-year, their writing began to demonstrate simple sentences, familiar spelling patterns, and ideas that were largely focused on their personal world.

Interacting with the junior and intermediate students was always a treat. I modeled accountable talk that made students ponder and think deeply about the purpose of their writing and whether their piece was meeting the needs of the reader. Teachers appreciated my in-class discussions with students and soon learned about the principal's passion for reading and writing. My walk-throughs often became the focus of professional dialogue with teachers over lunch or in passing. Students quickly learned that one of the most effective ways to communicate to me was through purposeful writing. I received various writing pieces from my students, ranging from proposals for an air-band competition, persuasive letters for cafeteria tables, reports about how much garbage we consume, and jokes to be read for the morning announcements. I loved seeing how students conveyed their messages with conviction and I cherished every word that students put on paper. This was the fuel that ignited my passion for being a literacy principal. Perhaps most important of all was that students saw how I took the time to care deeply about their writing achievement.

Teacher Moderation

A major aspect of our Professional Learning Communities (PLCs) involved teacher moderation, an activity whereby teachers come together and collaboratively assess students' work. Because our data revealed gaps in writing, especially in our junior division, I worked closely with my junior PLC examining students' writing pieces. We established common writing assessments (Ontario Writing Assessment) and began to build a trusting and professional relationship among the team. During the moderation process, we conferred with each other and referred to anchors, rubrics, curriculum documents, and various support materials. Regular teacher moderation sessions throughout the year enabled our teams to

- assess students' writing in a consistent manner
- determine patterns and trends
- set goals for student progress
- investigate and share key instructional strategies
- plan and deliver next steps for instruction
- re-assess to measure students' writing progress and determine the effectiveness of targeted strategies
- set goals for class and school improvement

PRODUCTIVE CONFLICT

At one of our moderation sessions mid way through the year, Grade 4 teacher Karen commented on my decision about a student's writing piece. She flat-out disagreed with my judgment about the students' knowledge of the text form. She calmly said to me, "Mary, I don't think he's a level 3 (the provincial standard). I disagree because his piece is not as strong as the level-3 anchor ..." I was taken aback. No one had ever challenged my judgment before. After all, I was the principal and instructional leader. It took me a while to register her rationale, but then I realized that it pushed my thinking up a notch. Karen's comment forced me to delve deeper into the criteria we were assessing, and our entire team was suddenly immersed in a rich dialogue about what makes a level 3, and what this student needed to move forward into a solid level-3 range. Teacher moderation enabled us to compare, confirm, and adjust judgments about students' work, establishing a consistent understanding of the levels of achievement and students' gaps in learning.

When Karen challenged me during that teacher moderation session, I recognized that we had established a culture that was open to differing ideas, in which we were equitably heard, respected, and unafraid to voice our opinions for the purpose of attaining high student achievement. Productive conflict was deeply embedded in our PLC discussions. Our teacher moderation sessions became dynamic learning experiences because we gained deeper insights into how students learn to write and worked together to plan precise next steps.

EXAMPLE OF THE MODERATION PROCESS

Write your legend here. How the Duck :: got it's webbed feet.

Along time ago ducks had feet like chickens. They loved the water and spend most of the time playing in the shallow water at the edge of the shore. But the water was coming more and more polluted each day from the people in the Village because they did not have indoor washrooms. All of the sewage ran into the lake. Alot of the animals died from infections from the contaminations in the lake. The ducks didn't die some became ill but they recovered. There feet however became infected. A strange kind of fungus started to grow between there toes. It did not go away and over the years it continue to grow farther down there toes. Then the stranges thing began to happen. The baby ducks were born with there toes webbed together down to the frist joint.

The process continued. With each new generation of baby ducks, the toes were becoming more and more webbed. This might have had something to do with the fact that the ducks were spending most of there time swimming in the polluted water and the foot fungus continued to grow and be passed down until all signs of chicken feet were gone. And that's how the duck got it's webbed feet.

During the moderation process, our PLC carefully read the student's writing piece. We assessed the student's writing through the four categories outlined in the Ontario Curriculum Achievement Chart. The following demonstrates our team's reasoning used in the assessment of each category. Our decisions involved professional dialogue referring to the rubric, anchors, and rationales.

Knowledge and Understanding   Level 4
Drew demonstrates thorough knowledge and understanding of a narrative text form, providing details that relate to the main event with a high degree of effectiveness (e.g., *All of the sewage ran into the lake. A lot of the animals died from infections from the contaminations in the lake.*). The story contains all the characteristics of a narrative, as well as the development of sequential events that lead to an ending with a high degree of clarity and focus (e.g., *And that's how the duck got it's webbed feet.*)

Thinking   Level 4
Drew generates ideas with a high degree of effectiveness, and there are many thorough details in the story that support the ideas being developed (e.g., *A strange kind of fungus started to grow between there toes.*). The writing

demonstrates a high degree of creative thinking (*e.g. The process continued. With each new generation of baby duck, the toes were becoming more and more webbed*)

Communication   Level 3

Drew expresses ideas clearly and organizes ideas logically in this narrative. She communicates effectively to the reader. The writing demonstrates the purpose to entertain with considerable effectiveness (e.g., *Then the strangest thing began to happen*). Drew makes effective use of vocabulary and conventions, varies sentence length, and makes few spelling errors. To make this a level 4, voice and tone can be stronger. Drew should communicate the mood of the narrative through exclamation marks, and more descriptive word choice.

Application   Level 4

Drew makes connections among the topic (how ducks got webbed feet), personal experiences (e.g., "*But the water was coming more and more polluted each day*"), and life situations with considerable effectiveness. Drew is able to transfer her understanding of contaminated water and its impact on animals to enhance her narrative (e.g., *The ducks didn't die some became ill but they recovered.*)

Next Steps

Drew needs to be immersed in rich literature that has a distinct style, voice, and tone. She will study the elements of writing such as descriptive word choice, metaphoric language, and similes, and how they create a writer's own voice. Drew's teacher decided that she should focus on three authors and their distinct techniques. Drew will examine how Chris Van Allsberg creates mysterious moods, how Eve Bunting's style is precise yet strong and emotional, and how Cynthia Rylant crafts warm and feel good stories based on relationships and family. Drew will select a mentor text that will support her voice when writing. She will dissect the mentor text and use it to support her narrative writing. Drew will also be grouped with other students that require a similar focus through small group shared lessons. In two weeks, Drew will be assessed through another narrative. With precise and targeted teaching, we expect improvements in how Drew communicates her voice, style, and tone to enhance her writing.

As a team, we became more cohesive and learned to pinpoint where students required further support. We shared our effective literacy practices and learned that our teaching responsibility went beyond our own classroom. Teacher moderation enabled our PLC members to share the responsibility of teaching literacy to all students. I welcomed and fostered productive conflict because it promoted equitable practices by improving consistency and accountability.

School-Wide Common Structures

Toward the end of the second term, our staff worked on school-wide shared expectations that would be evident in all classrooms. Collectively as a school we valued literacy activities as joyful, functional, and always meaningful. We agreed on common practices that would be evident in each and every classroom. As a staff we felt strongly that students needed to be immersed in these common structures, research-based strategies that supported teaching and learning. It is important to note that this is a beginning checklist, and we continue to refine and add as our journey of inquiry continues.

- Reading and writing strategies are posted on anchor charts. Teachers model strategies explicitly. Students also contribute to the anchor charts through shared lessons. Students readily access them and refer to them to support their literacy work. This ensures that the classroom has ownership of the strategies and they are relevant to students' learning. These are not commercially produced posters.
- Various text forms are evident in the classroom as they are taught throughout the year. Writing is taught with the understanding of purpose and audience. Students have experience with the following major text forms: recount, narrative, procedure, persuasive, report, explanation, and poetry.
- The following reading strategies are evident in each classroom. Each strategy is explicitly taught, maintained, extended. Some require more in-depth teaching than others, depending on grade, students' readiness, and zone of development:
  - activating prior knowledge (schema)
  - determining important information
  - making connections
  - questioning
  - visualizing
  - summarizing
  - predicting
  - inferring
  - synthesizing
  - evaluating and monitoring
  - repairing understanding
  - Texts of all types are evident including media literacy.
  - All students see their work displayed.
- Rich literature is a major aspect of every classroom. Texts are strategically selected to teach specific elements in writing and reading.
- An uninterrupted literacy block involves the interconnected opportunities between reading and writing. When we read, we must think like a writer, and when we write, we must think like a reader.
- Strategies are taught through the components of balanced literacy: modeled, shared, guided, and independent practice. Interactive writing is part of the Kindergarten to Grade 2 programs.
- Teachers plan with the end in mind. Teachers know exactly what students are expected to demonstrate independently by the end of a unit. The series of learning activities are scaffolded over a period of time. The teacher gradually releases responsibility onto the student.
- A question chart (Q chart) is evident throughout all classrooms, ensuring that we focus on higher-order questions for both students and teachers. Teachers focus on high-level thinking so that that students go beyond regurgitation of facts. Students are challenged through meaningful open-ended learning experiences.

Conclusion

During the last six years, we have had the opportunity to talk with administrators and school leaders in different districts throughout North America who have read and commented on our book *The Literacy Principal*. We have observed their heartfelt recognition of the primary place in schools of literacy success for every student. In this new version of *The Literacy Principal*, we wanted to add support to this educational movement by revising the book and presenting current research, educational books and websites, and new influential voices. School leaders, whose jobs have become more influential and significant than ever before, need to meet achievement targets and increased curriculum responsibilities. In tackling the complicated topic of how to lead, support, and assess literacy initiatives, we were given strength from the research and practice in two important, but seemingly incommensurable, fields — school change and literacy education. As Michael Fullan so aptly expressed it in his original Foreword, "Literacy education, like any innovation, requires change leadership. "

All of us involved in literacy education recognize the multiplicity of needs of different readers and writers in different settings, as well as understanding the importance of an integrated approach to change through common goals and understandings, shared leadership, and a motivation to improve the literacy standards of *all* children. New initiatives, such as teacher mentorship programs, the use of literacy coaches in schools and districts, and extensive and extended professional development, have changed how schools are meeting the needs of students. We hope that the new information and voices in this book offer support for the planning, implementing, and assessing of your school's literacy programs. Also, by reflecting on the comments of such fine educators as Carol Rolheiser, Kathryn Broad, Steven Reid, Mary Reid, Susan Schwartz, Jeannie Wilson, Jim Strachan, Lea Pelletier, Cathy Costello, Lyn Sharratt, Enrique Puig, Kathy Froelich, Theresa Licitra, Mark Federman, Linda Cameron, and Gwen McCutcheon, whose voices inform and illuminate our discussion, we hope that we have placed literacy theory in a practical and authentic light.

Literacy growth for all children is a powerful goal for schools to try to achieve. And, we now know that it takes everyone in the school to make this outcome a possibility. Your stewardship in this vital aspect of education is at the heart of the process — your leadership in guiding teachers and parents in developing an effective literacy program will determine its success. We celebrate your continuing commitment to the goal of having all children become "print powerful" as they participate in nurturing and supportive literacy-based schools.

District-Wide Strategies to Raise Student Achievement in Literacy and Numeracy

Carol Campbell, Michael Fullan, and Avis Glaze

The Effective District Strategies project began in summer 2005. The purpose of the project was to identify districts in Ontario that are demonstrating improvements in literacy and numeracy and to evaluate the strategies, actions, and outcomes associated with such improvements. The Literacy and Numeracy Secretariat is working in partnership with boards across Ontario to achieve this result. This project is part of the Secretariat's work to unlock potential for learning by sharing successful practices. The project has, however, not just focused on high-achieving boards, but also on growth and improvement in both lower- and higher-performing boards. This has enabled the Secretariat to identify effective practices for districts at different stages of improvement and achievement levels and to learn lessons across the range of contexts and experiences in Ontario. The case study districts do not offer exact blueprints for success, but rather provide concrete examples of what effective strategies look like in practice. The project's research questions focused around three key areas of enquiry. We list these here to enable the reader to reflect on how you would answer these questions in relation to your own context:

1. **District's Strategy and Actions**

    - What is the district's approach to improving student achievement in literacy and numeracy?
    - What is the main purpose driving this approach and what are the goals to be achieved?
    - What strategies and actions are in place on a district-wide basis?
    - What is the structure and operation of the district to support a focus on student achievement?
    - What are the roles and responsibilities of key individual postholders within the district?

2. **Connections Between District and Schools**

    - Has a shared focus on literacy and/or numeracy been fostered across all schools?
    - At the school level, what initiatives and actions have taken place to improve student achievement in literacy and numeracy?
    - What is the relationship between the district and schools in supporting literacy/numeracy improvements?
    - How does the district challenge all schools to improve?
    - What types of support do schools receive from the district?
    - How is professional learning shared within and across schools?

3. **Impact of District's Strategies and Actions and Future Developments**

    - Overall, how effective is the district's approach to improving student achievement in literacy and numeracy?
    - What specific strategies and actions have been most effective?
    - What have been the main difficulties encountered and how have these been addressed?
    - How can improvements become sustainable?
    - What further developments are planned or required to improve student achievement district-wide?
    - What has been the key learning for the district in improving student achievement in literacy and/or numeracy?
    - What lessons have been learned of relevance to other districts and/or for province-wide reform?

(Campbell, Fullan & Glaze, 2006)

Leading Toward Literacy

Principles for Building a Literacy Community

CONNECTING THE HOME, THE SCHOOL, AND THE COMMUNITY

We need to integrate the home and school worlds of every student so that parents and caregivers can work alongside the school in supporting literacy for all children.

UNDERSTANDING BOYS AND GIRLS AS READERS AND WRITERS

We need to understand and appreciate the developing characteristics and behaviors of individual boys and girls in a variety of literacy situations, and recognize the effect of gender and social issues on their developing literacy lives.

PROVIDING LITERACY MODELS FOR BOYS AND GIRLS

We need to ensure that boys have male literacy models in their homes, in their schools, and in the community, so that they will associate reading and writing activities, both on the page and onscreen, with other boys and male adults in their lives.

CONSTRUCTING A READER

We need to understand how a reader is constructed, what factors affect a child's literacy development, and how a child could see himself/herself as a literate member of society.

GIVING STUDENTS CHOICE AND OWNERSHIP IN THEIR READING

We need to provide students with a wide variety of resources that they want to read and at different reading levels. We need to rethink the place of the literary canon in literacy development and bring the students' outside reading inside school.

ACKNOWLEDGING THE IMPACT OF COMPUTER TECHNOLOGY ON BOYS' AND GIRLS' LITERACY

We need to accept the literacy revolution brought on by the computer and information technology and help boys and girls to become discriminating and critical users.

Helping Boys and Girls Become Print Powerful

PROVIDING SUPPORT FOR THOSE WHO ARE AT RISK IN LITERACY

We need to provide direct instruction and appropriate resources at appropriate levels for boys and girls who are non-readers, limited readers, or reluctant readers, so that they can fully enter the literacy world as proficient readers and writers.

LETTING BOYS AND GIRLS IN ON THE SECRETS OF PROFICIENT READERS

We need to share with boys and girls the strategies that proficient readers use to make sense of difficult texts or unfamiliar genres or formats.

HELPING BOYS AND GIRLS TO DEEPEN AND EXTEND COMPREHENSION

We need to encourage boys and girls to make meaning when they read by connecting the text to their personal experiences and feelings, to other texts, and to past and present world events.

CREATING A VIABLE LITERACY STRUCTURE FOR BOYS AND GIRLS

We need to create a structure for literacy that connects boys' and girls' homes, schools, and outside worlds, so that we can motivate and support boys and girls in becoming independent and proficient lifelong readers and writers.

Assisting Boys and Girls in Becoming Writers

HELPING STUDENTS TO DEVELOP WRITING TOPICS THAT MATTER

We need to develop authentic reasons for having boys and girls write, so they will value opportunities for writing for a variety of functions and for different audiences. We need to help students find reasons and methods for revising and editing their written work, and then offer them ways of sharing the final drafts.

HELPING STUDENTS TO SHARE AND SHAPE STORIES FROM THEIR LIVES

We need to promote the recalling, the sharing, and the shaping of their life stories as useful resources for reading and writing.

USING DRAMA AS A SOURCE FOR READING AND WRITING

We need to develop drama units in which students can express and reflect upon their ideas and feelings artistically, cooperatively, and safely.

REVEALING AND UNDERSTANDING EMOTIONS THROUGH POETRY

We need to incorporate poetry into the literacy lives of students to open up reflective and emotional responses, and to demonstrate the power of language.

HELPING STUDENTS BUILD WORD MUSCLES

We need to find effective teaching strategies for developing spelling and language strengths in students' written projects, so that they see themselves as competent writers.

Structuring Literacy Events for Students

MODELING AND DEMONSTRATING LITERACY STRATEGIES

We need to model and demonstrate specific literacy strategies so that students can learn the secrets of how successful readers and writers work.

RECOGNIZING INQUIRY AS A CENTRAL MOTIVATION FOR READING AND WRITING

We need to recognize inquiry as the basis for drawing students into authentic reading and writing activities using different genres of non-fiction resources; we also need to provide opportunities to build upon their interests in informational and instructional modes as resources and topics for writing.

DEMYSTIFYING ASSESSMENT AND EVALUATION PROCESSES

We need to develop assessment strategies and use evaluation procedures to enable students to recognize their strengths and uncover their problems. We can then design useful instruction for supporting their literacy growth.

BUILDING LITERACY AND LITERATURE RESOURCES FOR STUDENTS

We need to find resources on the page and onscreen for all kinds of readers, from beginning readers to gifted, mature readers, and for readers with different backgrounds and interests.

Afterword

I have spent most of my life alongside school principals, as a student for thirteen years (and since we moved house almost every year, I met a lot of them), as a classroom teacher in three different schools for ten years, as a language arts consultant for six years, and as a teacher educator in a faculty of education for the rest of my career. In each of these situations, I seldom felt part of a reciprocal relationship; these school leaders always seemed in a position of absolute authority, and I felt completely subservient.

As a child, I respected all of the principals that led the schools I attended, from Mr. Van Horne, who wore a fresh flower in his lapel every day, to Mr. Tilden, who allowed me to answer the school phone in his absence. But then, I was a mousy, academic child who was never sent to the office for rule infractions, and, as a result, I saw these leaders (they were all males) as solemn figureheads who seldom, if ever, entered a classroom and who were never seen teaching (or reading!).

As a young teacher, this recognition of their power status stayed with me, and I carefully maintained a distant and professional demeanor with each of the four men under whose leadership I served — Roy Howard, Ted Humphries, Roy Ito, and Ivan Thompson. I respected them all. However, during those years, curriculum development appeared not to be part of their mandate, for we had several subject consultants who supported our professional development. I was a complex and sometimes difficult teacher, and these men showed great patience and faith in my efforts to learn to teach, and I was given free rein to invent my own programs. However, without the mentoring from consultants, such as the nurturing English supervisor Bill Moore, I would have wandered off in all directions, with my children lost in the literacy woods.

When I became a reading consultant, I quickly recognized the impact of the principal on the culture of the school. When you visit a hundred schools in a supporting role for teachers, your effectiveness is determined to a large degree by how you are welcomed by the school leader. What context have they established for your participation in the programs and the initiatives of their schools? What long-term goals have they developed with their staffs that involve your role as a literacy consultant? Who I could be in a school was in their hands. Where I could make a contribution depended on the framework that had been put in place, and the principal's role in the culture of the school determined our progress together. This change process has now been documented through Michael Fullan's work, and we consequently have solid grounds for establishing systems of effective school growth.

In working with schools as a teacher educator in a faculty of education, we depend on our relationships with schools for organizing our preservice students for their practicum placements, and I notice how the role of the principal has begun to change. In recent years I have met men and women leaders with deep interests in literacy learning, and many who have taken methodology courses and in-service sessions in the different aspects of helping youngsters become readers and writers. As well, in their new roles, these leaders have become aware of how school leadership needs to function if teachers are to be supported in meaningful ways toward professional growth. I now feel much more like a team member, all of us working toward the education of children.

These days I find myself working often with groups of principals and school leaders throughout North America, and I am strengthened by their anecdotes of their schoolwide successes in literacy endeavors, from achievement tests to worldwide computer network links. Together, we have learned that skill-drill is not enough; we know that young people need real reasons for reading and writing in order to build a vision of what literacy can do for them in their lives, alongside those abilities required to fully participate as readers and writers. Still, in desperation from directives from headquarters or pressure groups, we sometimes find ourselves once again searching for the magic program that will ensure literacy success for every student in our school, only to realize that solid, long-range and school-wide professional development is the appropriate answer.

My perspective of the role of school leadership has altered through the writing of this book. Jennifer Rowsell, the co-author, brought a world of wisdom to our writing sessions and to the interviews we conducted with several of the excellent literacy principals in our area. Her research and her inquiries resulted in the sharing of so much information about the role of literacy-based school change, and deepened my own understanding of the influence of school leaders in the reading and writing programs we develop for our students.

I celebrate those educators who lead from within the circle that embraces all students. On a final note, I defer to Shelley Harwayne in *Going Public* on the role of teachers and administrators as models and mentors of literacy-based school change:

> Principals, as well as teachers, can be models, in fact they 'must' be models. How can we ask students to lead literate lives if we don't? Of course, I don't take care of my own literacy because I'm trying to inspire anyone, I do it because reading and writing are two of life's pleasures. I work hard; I deserve them.

David Booth
Ontario Institute for Studies in Education, University of Toronto

Resources

Adams, Marilyn, et al. (1998) *Phonemic Awareness in Young Children.* Baltimore, MD: Brookes.

Allen, Janet (2007) *Inside Words: Tools for Teaching Academic Vocabulary, Grades 4–12.* Portland, ME: Stenhouse.

Allen, Jennifer (2006) *Becoming a Literacy Leader: Supporting Learning and School Change.* Portland, ME: Stenhouse.

Allington, Richard L. (2006) *What Really Matters for Struggling Readers: Designing Research-based Programs,* 2nd ed. Boston, MA: Allyn & Bacon.

Atwell, Nancie (2007) *The Reading Zone.* New York, NY: Scholastic.

Barton, D. & Hamilton, M. (1998) *Local Literacies: Reading and Writing in One Community.* London, UK: Routledge.

Beers, Kylene (2003) *When Kids Can't Read, What Teachers Can Do.* Portsmouth, NH: Heinemann.

Black, P. & Wiliam, D. (1998) "Assessment and Classroom Learning" *Assessment in Education,* 5 (1), 7–75.

Bodiam, M.; Coulter, J.; Doctorow, R.; McGowan, H. & Reid, M. (2007) *Second Edition, CASI — Comprehension, Attitude, Strategies, Interests — Reading Assessment, Grades 4 to 8.* Scarborough, ON: Nelson Learning.

Bodrova, E. & Leong, D. J. (1996) *Tools of the Mind: The Vygotskian Approach to Early Childhood Education.* Englewood Cliffs, NJ: Merrill/ Prentice-Hall.

Bomer, Randy (1995) *Time for Reading: Crafting Literate Lives in Middle and High School.* Portsmouth, NH: Heinemann.

Booth, David (1998) *Guiding the Reading Process: Techniques and Strategies for Successful Instruction in K–8 Classrooms.* Markham, ON: Pembroke.

Booth, David (2000) *Even Hockey Players Read.* Markham, ON: Pembroke.

Booth, David (2001) *Reading and Writing in the Middle Years.* Markham, ON: Pembroke.

Booth, David (2006) *Reading Doesn't Matter Anymore.* Markham, ON: Pembroke.

Booth, David & Lundy, Kathleen (2007) *Boosting Literacy with Graphic Novels.* Austin, TX: Steck-Vaughn.

Booth, David & Lundy, Kathleen (2007) *In Graphic Detail: Using Graphic Novels in the Classroom.* Markham, ON: Scholastic Canada.

Booth, David; Green, Joan & Booth, Jack (2004) *I Want to Read.* Oakville, ON: Rubicon.

Bouchard, David, with Wendy Sutton (2001) *The Gift of Reading.* Victoria, BC: Orca.

Boucher, Irene; Dye, Lesleigh & Reid, Steven (2003) *Project Literacy: A Handbook for the Early Years.* Markham, ON: Scholastic Canada.

Calkins, Lucy & Bellino, Lydia (1997) *Raising Lifelong Learners: A Parent's Guide.* Reading, MA: Addison-Wesley.

Campbell, Carol; Fullan, Michael & Glaze, Avis (2006) *Case Study Report: Unlocking Potential for Learning: Effective District-Wide Strategies to Raise Student Achievement in Literacy and Numeracy.* Toronto, ON: Literacy and Numeracy Secretariat.

Carrington, V. (2006) *Rethinking Middle Years: Early Adolescents, Schooling, and Digital Culture.* London, UK: Allen & Unwin.

Charlton, Beth Critchley (2005) *Informal Assessment Strategies.* Markham, ON: Pembroke.

Church, Susan (2005) *The Principal Difference.* Markham, ON: Pembroke.

CIERA (Center for the Improvement of Early Reading Achievement) (2000)*An Analysis of Early Literacy Assessments Used for Instruction.* University of Michigan.

Clay, Marie M. (1993) *An Observation Survey of Early Literacy Achievement.* Auckland, NZ: Heinemann Education.

Comber, B. & Nixon, H. (2004) "Children re-read and re-write their neighborhoods: critical literacies and identity work" in Janet Evans (Ed.) *Literacy Moves On: Popular Culture, New Technologies and Critical Literacy in the Elementary Classroom* (127–148). Portsmouth, NH: Heinemann.

Cope, B. & Kalantzis, M. (2000) *Multiliteracies.* London, UK: Routledge.

Cotton, Kathleen (2003) *Principals and Student Achievement: What the Research Says.* Alexandria, VA: ASCD.

Crain, William (2003) *Reclaiming Childhood: Letting Children Be Children in Our Achievement-Oriented Society.* New York, NY: Henry Holt and Co.

Crevola, C.A. & Hill, P.W. (1998) *Children's Literacy Success Strategy: An Overview.* Melbourne, AU: Catholic Education Office.

Cummins, Jim (1996) *Negotiating Identities: Education for Empowerment in a Diverse Society,* 2nd ed. Toronto, ON: Ontario Institute for Studies in Education.

Cunningham, Patricia (1995) *The Phonics They Use.* Portsmouth, NH: Heinemann.

Cunningham, Patricia; Moore, Sharon; Cunningham, James & Moore, David (1995) *Reading and Writing in Elementary Classrooms: Strategies and Observations,* 3rd ed. New York, NY: Longman.

Daniels, Harvey (2002) *Literature Circles: Voice and Choice in Book Clubs and Reading Groups.* Portland, ME: Stenhouse.

Davies, Anne (2000) *Making Classroom Assessment Work.* Merville, BC: Connections.

Davies, J. & Merchant, G. (2007) "Looking from the Inside-Out: Academic Blogging as New Literacy" in M. Knobel & C. Lankshear *New Literacies Sampler.* New York, NY: Peter Lang.

Davis, Carol & Yang, Alice (2005) *Parents and Teachers Working Together.* Greenfield, MA: NEFC.

Dixon-Krauss, L. (1996) *Vygotsky in the Classroom: Mediated literacy Instruction and Assessment.* Boston, MA: Allyn & Bacon.

Dorn, Linda J. & Soffos, Carla (2001) *Scaffolding Young Writers: A Writers' Workshop Approach.* Portland, ME: Stenhouse.

Downey, English, Frase, Poston & Steffy (2004)*The Three-Minute Walk-Through: Changing School Supervisory Practice One Teacher at a Time.* Thousand Oaks, CA: Sage.

Duckworth, Eleanor (1996) *"The Having of Wonderful Ideas" & Other Essays on Teaching and Learning,* 2nd ed. New York, NY: Teachers College Press.

Dyson, A.H. (2003) *The Brothers and Sisters Learn to Write: Popular Literacies in Childhood and School Cultures.* New York, NY: Teachers College Press.

Easley, Shirley-Dale & Mitchell, Kay (2003) *Portfolios Matter: What, Where, When, Why and How to Use Them.* Markham, ON: Pembroke.

Edge, Karen; Rolheiser, Carol & Fullan, Michael (2001) "Case Studies of Literacy-Driven Educational Change: The Toronto District School Board's Early Years Literacy Project" Toronto District School Board.

Education Department of Western Australia (EDWA) (1993) *First Steps*. Portsmouth, NH: Heinemann.

Elkind, D. (2007) *The Power of Play: How Spontaneous, Imaginative Activities Lead to Happier, Healthier Children*. Cambridge, MA: Da Capo Press.

Elmore, Richard (2005)*Bridging the Gap for Accountability and Achievement*. ASCD Conference, April.

Fay, Kathleen & Whaley, Suzanne (2004) *Becoming One Community: Reading and Writing with English Language Learners*. Portland, ME: Stenhouse.

Fisher, Ros; Lewis, Maureen & Davis, Bernie (2000) "Progress and Performance in National Literacy Strategy Classrooms" *Journal of Research in Reading*, 23 (1), 256–266.

Fletcher, Ralph (2006) *Boy Writers: Reclaiming their Voices*. Portland, ME: Stenhouse.

Foster, Graham & Marasco, Toni L. (2007) *Exemplars: Your Best Resource to Improve Student Writing*. Markham, ON: Pembroke.

Fountas, Irene & Pinnell, Gay Su (2001) *Guiding Readers and Writers Grades 3–6*. Portsmouth, NH: Heinemann.

Fountas, Irene & Pinnell, Gay Su (2007) *Teaching for Comprehension and Fluency K–8*. Portsmouth, NH: Heinemann.

Fox, D. (2001) "No More Random Acts of Teaching" *Leadership* (Nov–Dec): 14–17.

Freire, P. & Macedo, D. (1987) *Literacy: Reading the Word and the World*. South Hadley, MA: Bergen and Garvey.

Fullan, Michael (2006) *Turnaround Leadership*. New York, NY: John Wiley and Sons.

Fullan, Michael (2007) *The New Meaning of Educational Change*, 3rd ed. New York, NY: Teachers College Press.

Gallas, Karen (2003) *Imagination and Literacy*. New York, NY: Teachers College Press.

Gambrell, L.; Morrow, L. & Pressley, M. (2007) *Best Practices in Literacy Instruction*, 3rd ed. New York, NY: Guilford.

Gentry, J. Richard (2007) *The New Science of Beginning Reading and Writing*. Portsmouth, NH: Heinemann.

Gonzales, N.; Moll, L. & Amanti C. (eds) (2005) *Funds of Knowledge: Theorizing Practices in Households, Communities and Classrooms*. Rahway, NJ: Lawrence Erlbaum.

Harvey, Stephanie & Goudvis, Anne (2007) *Strategies that Work, 2nd edition: Teaching Comprehension for Understanding and Engagement*. Portland, ME: Stenhouse.

Harwayne, Shelley (1999) *Going Public: Priorities & Practice at the Manhattan New School*. Portsmouth, NH: Heinemann.

Harwayne, Shelley (2000) *Lifetime Guarantees: Toward Ambitious Literacy Teaching*. Portsmouth, NH: Heinemann.

Heath, S.B. (1983) *Ways with Words: Language, Life, and Work in Communities and Classrooms*. Cambridge, UK: Cambridge University Press.

Hindley, Joanne (1995) *In the Company of Children*. Portland, ME: Stenhouse.

Hurry, Jane (2000) "Intervention Strategies to Support Pupils with Difficulties in Literacy During Key Stage 1. Review of Research." London, UK: Institute of Education, University of London.

Jobe, Ron & Dayton-Sakari, Mary (1999) *Reluctant Readers: Connecting Students and Books for Successful Reading Experiences*. Markham, ON: Pembroke.

Johnston, Peter (1997) *Knowing Literacy*. Portland, ME: Stenhouse.

Johnston, Peter (1997) *Running Records: A Self-Tutoring Guide*. Portland, ME: Stenhouse.

Knobel, M. & Lankshear, C. (2007) *A New Literacies Sampler*. New York, NY: Peter Lang.

Kosnik, Clare (1998)*Spelling in a Balanced Literacy Program.* Scarborough, ON: ITP Nelson.

Kress, G. (1997). *Before Writing: Rethinking The Paths to Literacy.* London, UK: Routledge.

Leithwood, Kenneth, et al. (2006) *Teaching for Deep Understanding.* Thousand Oaks, CA: Corwin Press

Leithwood, Kenneth; Fullan, Michael & Laing, Pauline (2002) "Towards the Schools We Need: OISE/UT Researchers Offer Advice to New Premier on How to Revitalize the Education System" *The Bulletin,* 55th Year, Number 17, April 22, 20.

Leu, D. & Coiro, J. (2004) "New Literacies for New Times: Why and How the Literacy Community Needs to Rethink Its Mission" *WSRA Journal.* Volume 44, Number 5. Spring, 3–7.

Lipton, L.; Wellman, B. & Humbard, C. (2003) *Mentoring Matters: A Practical Guide to Learning-focused Relationships,* 2nd ed. Sherman, CT: Mira Vira, LLC.

Louv, Richard (2006) *Last Child in the Woods: Saving Our Children from Nature-Deficit Disorder.* New York, NY: Workman.

Luke, A. (2004) "Two takes on the critical" in B. Norton & K. Toohey, eds., *Critical Pedagogy and Language Learning.* Cambridge, UK: Cambridge University Press.

Lundy, Kathleen Gould (2004) *What Do I Do About the Kid Who...?* Markham, ON: Pembroke.

Lundy, Kathleen Gould (2007) *Leap into Literacy.* Markham, ON: Pembroke.

Luongo-Orlando, Katherine (2006) *Authentic Assessment: Designing Performance-Based Tasks.* Markham, ON: Pembroke.

Lyons, Carol & Pinnell, Gay Su (2001) *Systems for Change in Literacy Education: A Guide to Professional Development.* Portsmouth, NH: Heinemann.

MacGinitie, Walter H. et al. (2000) *Gates-MacGinitie Reading Test (GMRT), Forms S & T.,* 4th ed. Scarborough, ON: Nelson Thomson Learning.

Mascall, Blair; Fullan, Michael & Rolheiser, Carol (2002) "The Challenges of Coherence and Capacity: Case Studies on the Implementation of Early Literacy in York Region." Toronto, ON: York Region District School Board.

Mckenna, Frank (2007) *Literacy Matters: A Call for Action.* Toronto, ON: Toronto Dominion Financial Group.

Melton, Glennon Doyle & Greene, Amy H. (2007) *Test Talk: Integrating Test Preparation into Reading Workshop.* Portland, ME: Stenhouse.

Mulroney, Catherine (2002) "Testing The Unseen Curriculum." *The Toronto Star.* May 13.

Murphy, Joseph (2004) *Leadership for Literacy.* Thousand Oaks, CA: Corwin Press.

Nichols, Sharon L. & Berliner, David C. (2007) *Collateral Damage: How High-Stakes Testing Corrupts America's Schools.* Cambridge, MA: Harvard Education Press.

Pahl, Kate & Rowsell, Jennifer (2005) *Literacy and Education: Understanding the New Literacies Studies in the Classroom.* London, UK: Sage.

Prothero, Brenda & Hilker, Doug (2005) *Reality Check: Assessing for Achievement.* Oakville, ON: Rubicon.

Puig, E. A. & Froelich, K. S. (2007) *The Literacy Coach: Guiding in the Right Direction.* Boston, MA: Allyn & Bacon.

Purkey, W. & Novak, J. (1984) *Inviting School Success.* Belmont, CA: Wadsworth.

Ontario Ministry of Education (2006) *New Teacher Induction Program Resource Handbooks.* Available at: http://www.edu.gov.on.ca/eng/teacher/resources.html

Reid, S. & Reid, M. (2008) *Ontario Writing Assessment.* Scarborough, ON: Nelson Learning.

Robb, Laura (2000) *Redefining Staff Development: A Collaborative Model for Teachers and Administrators.* Portsmouth, NH: Heinemann.

Robbins, Pam & Harvey, Alvy (2004) *The New Principal's Fieldbook.* Alexandria, VA: ASCD.

Rosenblatt, L. (2005) *Making Meaning With Texts.* Portsmouth, NH: Heinemann.

Routman, Regie (2000) *Conversations: Strategies for Teaching, Learning and Evaluating.* Portsmouth, NH: Heinemann.

Rowsell, Jennifer (2006) *Family Literacy Experiences.* Markham, ON: Pembroke.

Schon, D.A. (1983) *The Reflective Practitioner.* New York, NY: Basic Books.

Schwartz, Susan & Pollishuke, Mindy (2002) *Creating the Dynamic Classroom: A Handbook for Teachers.* Toronto, ON: Irwin.

Scott, Ruth (2007) *Knowing Words: Creating Word-Rich Classrooms.* Scarborough, ON: Nelson.

Sharratt, Lyn & Fullan, Michael (2005) "The School District That Did the Right Things Right" Available at www.oise.utoronto.ca.

Shirran, Alex (2006) *Evaluating Students: How Teachers Justify and Defend their Marks to Parents, Students & Principals.* Markham, ON: Pembroke.

Snow, Catherine, et al. (2005) *Knowledge to Support the Teaching of Reading.* San Francisco, CA: John Wiley and Sons.

Stead, Tony (2001) *Is That a Fact? Teaching Nonfiction Writing K–3.* Portland, ME: Stenhouse.

Stead, Tony (2005) *Reality Checks.* Portland, ME: Stenhouse.

Strachan, J. (2007) "Job Embedded Learning for Beginning Teachers" in *Beyond PD Days: Teachers' Work and Learning in Canada.* Toronto, ON: Ontario Teachers Federation

Street, B.V. (1984) *Literacy in Theory and Practice.* Cambridge, UK: Cambridge University Press.

Strickland, D. & Alvermann (2004) *Bridging the Literacy Achievement Gap.* New York, NY: Teacher's College Press.

Strickland, Dorothy; Ganske, Kathy & Monroe, Joanne (2001) *Supporting Struggling Readers and Writers: Strategies for Classroom Intervention 3–6.* Portland, ME: Stenhouse.

Swartz, Larry (2002) *The New Dramathemes.* Markham, ON: Pembroke.

Sweeney, Diane (2003) *Learning Along the Way: Professional Development by and for Teachers.* Portland, ME: Stenhouse.

Szymusiak, Karen & Sibberson, Franki (2001) *Beyond Leveled Books: Supporting Transitional Readers in Grades 2–5.* Portland, ME: Stenhouse.

Taylor, Denny (1997) *Many Families, Many Literacies.* Portsmouth, NH: Heinemann.

Tharp, R.G. & Gallimore, R. (1988) *Rousing Minds to Life: Teaching, Learning, and Schooling in Social Context.* Cambridge, UK: Cambridge University Press.

Toronto District School Board (2007) *Supporting Beginning Teachers.* Available at http://schools.tdsb.on.ca/asit/standards/btstart/index.asp

Toronto District School Board (2007) *Welcome to Teaching & Learning.* Available at http://schools.tdsb.on.ca/asit/standards/btstart/index.asp

Tovani, Cris (2000) *I Read It, But I Don't Get It: Comprehension Strategies for Adolescent Readers*. Portland, ME: Stenhouse.

Trehearne, Miriam (2001) "Balanced Literacy Programs + Early Intervention = Success for All." Calgary Board of Education.

Waters, J. T.; Marzano, R. J. & McNulty, B. A. (2003) *Balanced Leadership: What 30 Years of Research Tells Us about the Effect of Leadership on Student Achievement.* Aurora, CO: Mid-continent Research for Education and Learning.

Wiggins, Grant & McTighe, Jay (1998) *Understanding by Design.* Alexandria, VA:
    Association for Supervision & Curriculum Development

Wilhelm, Jeffrey (2004) *Engaging Readers and Writers with Inquiry.* Portsmouth, NH:
    Heinemann.

Wormeli, Rick (2006) *Fair Isn't Always Equal.* Portland, ME: Stenhouse.

Wormeli, Rick (2007) *Differentiation: From Planning to Practice.* Portland, ME: Stenhouse.

Wortman, Robert (1996) *Administrators Supporting School Change.* Portland, ME:
    Stenhouse.

York Region District School Board (2007) *Guidelines for Literacy — A Curriculum
    Expectations Document.*

Index